Qatar

The
Business Traveller's
Handbook

GAC®

Wherever you go

For GAC and UPS contact details and services please
see inner front and reverse covers.

Qatar
The Business Traveller's Handbook

First published in 2003 by
Interlink Books
An imprint of Interlink Publishing Group, Inc.
46 Crosby Street, Northampton, Massachusetts 01060
www.interlinkbooks.com

ISBN 1-56656-497-2

Copyright © Gorilla Guides, 2003

Library of Congress Cataloging-in-Publication Data available

The author and publisher have made every effort to ensure that the facts in this handbook are accurate and up-to-date. The reader is advised, however, to verify travel and visa arrangements with the appropriate consular office prior to departure. The author and publisher cannot accept any responsibility for loss, injury or inconvenience, however caused.

None of the maps in this book are designed to have any political significance.

Printed and bound in Singapore by Tien Wah Press

To request our complete 40-page full-color catalog, please call us toll free at 1-800-238-LINK, visit our website at www.interlinkbooks.com or send us an e-mail: info@interlinkbooks.com

PICTURE CREDITS: *Title page: Stacey International; p4: (t) Image Bank; p6: (t), (bl) John Herbert; p7: (b) John Herbert; all others are Stacey International*

Qatar

The Business Travellers' Handbook

David Chaddock

Above: The Emir's Palace in Doha, commanding the waterfront, is not so much a royal residence as the pivotal structure of modern government.

Below: Weaving, frequently from goat hair, is a traditional craft still practiced and decorative rugs are available in the local suqs.

Below: Qatar's heritage of music, both of song and instrument, is a development of ancient bedu tradition.

Above: the Sheraton Hotel, situated on Doha's sweeping bay, was the first international hotel on the peninsula.

Below left: 'Qatar maroon' is almost the national brand, cherished emblem of Qatar's emergence as an influential Islamic state.

Below right: the surveying and mapping of Qatar's desert region is a continuous process.

Above: the Arabian oryx, once on the brink of extinction, now flourishes as a herd in the Al Shahaniyah region of central Qatar, under a skilfully managed and monitored programme of mammal conservation.

Below: telecommunications have boomed in Qatar as elsewhere and communication today is easier than it has ever been.

Acknowledgements

I am indebted to several prime sources for factual information; these are the Qatar National Bank, the Law Offices of Dr. Najeeb bin Mohammed Al-Nuaimi, the Law Offices of Gebran Majdalany, the audit and accounting firm of Ernst & Young – Qatar, and the British Embassy Commercial Section.

My thanks also go to the many individuals, companies and organisations who have given me the opportunity to be a part of the tremendous developments of the Middle East and particularly the Gulf States. Only living the life has allowed the knowledge and experience to build to a point where committing it to paper has been almost as much fun as gaining it. The constant support of my wife and children through the easy, and not so easy, times is a given.

Qatar was one of two GCC states that I always said I wouldn't want to live in. After six years here, it is about to take over the other in length of residence! I have enjoyed them both. Qatar has a lot to offer the serious businessman with long-term goals in mind. I hope this guide will help achieve those goals.

DC 2003

CONTENTS

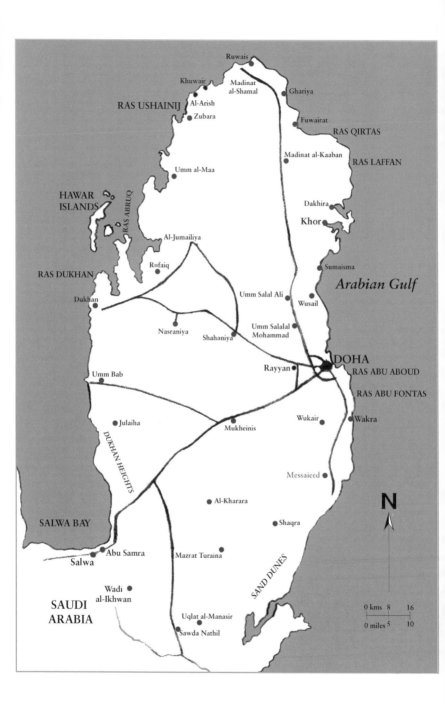

Qatar

1

Qatar yesterday and today

Qatar yesterday and today

A bird's-eye view of the nation, and the special features that distinguish it from other countries.

A condensed history.

The modern country.

A Brief History of Qatar

Qatar has become the richest nation in the world. Not bad for a place once described as 'a thumb sticking up out of the Gulf'. Admittedly, the definition of 'richest nation in the world' is based upon GNP per capita, and with a total population of only around 600,000 of which only 150,000 are citizens as opposed to expatriate residents, it is not difficult to achieve that distinction. Nevertheless, vast wealth derived from the exploitation of oil and immense natural gas reserves makes this small nation immensely rich, and its sound development plans give it the potential to become richer still.

The early history of the Gulf is essentially the story of the great Empires of Persia and Assyria in Mesopotamia – modern day Iraq. For them, the importance of the Gulf was the Gulf itself, its calm blue waters which allowed easy movement of goods and armies. And although influences came and went in the centuries of pre-Islamic history, the lingering architectural and genetic legacy of the region is that of the Persians.

Islam

In the early 7th century AD, the Prophet Muhammad emerged as an important force in Makkah, in what is now Saudi Arabia, acquiring a standing and following which alarmed the rulers of the city. In 622 AD (the first year of the Muslim calendar) Muhammad and his followers fled to Medina. There, in what has become one of the great Holy Cities, the Islamic religion was established. The word of God, as related to Muhammad, was embodied in the Holy Qur'an, a volume pieced together by Muhammad's followers after the Prophet's death in 632.

The region that included modern-day Qatar embraced Islam, under the benign authority of the Persian and Mesopotamian powers of the north. When the Abassids took control of the region in 750 AD and established their capital in Baghdad, the golden age of trade in the Gulf began. Merchants traded with India, China and East Africa, and the demand for pearls undoubtedly enriched the merchants of Qatar. Towns and settlements grew, the earliest known settlement being at Murwab near Zubara.

In the Gulf established itself as the new maritime power and soon gained control of trade. In 1498 the Portuguese

1

rounded the Cape of Good Hope, confirming a direct sea route to India, diverting trade from the Red Sea and the Gulf. With great brutality the Portuguese one by one took over the Arab ports of the Gulf coast, Hormuz itself being captured in 1515. By 1622 AD, the task of maintaining control of the Indian Ocean routes proved too much for the Portuguese, and Hormuz fell to the combined forces of Shah Abbas I of Persia, and Britain. All the forts that the Portuguese had snatched from the Arabs fell to the allies, and the Portuguese hold on the region was over.

Between 1630 and 1700 the Dutch East India Company and the English East India Company dominated trade in the Gulf.

While these great events were taking place, the region of Qatar was shaping itself into two distinct areas: the coastal, folk pursuing the fishing, pearling and trading activities that had sustained countless generations before them, and the bedouin pastoralist grazing the interior.

1

Wahhabis

Towards the end of the 18th century, a new religious force emerged. Muhammad Ibn Abdullah Al Wahhab developed an interpretation of Islam, whose followers became known as the Wahhabis. They called for a return to the more strict orthodox form of Islam. The teachings of Mohammed, as set down in the Qur'an, had been widely studied and variously interpreted over the years. The Wahhabis argued that it was time to get back to basics. This notion appealed to many tribes in the region, notably the Al Saud of the Riyadh area. The nature and tenets of Wahhabism also found favour with the Al-Thani tribe – prominent in the Qatar area. However, the new thinking did not appeal to the Al-Khalifas, the dominant tribe based in the Bahrain region. Hostilities broke out. Eventually the Al-Thani tribe established its Wahhabi outpost on the east coast of Qatar and in doing so formed the societal structure which survives to this day.

Al-Thanis

The British supported the Al-Thanis in their dispute with the Bahraini-based Al-Khalifas, and in 1868 an agreement was signed between the British Political Resident and the leader of the tribe, Mohammed Al-Thani. The treaty offered British protection in return for Al-Thani co-operation and consolidated the position of the Al-Thani tribe in the region, making them effectively the rulers of Qatar. The second result was that it locked Qatar and Britain into a quirky and special love-hate relationship.

This cosy relationship was soon to be tested when Ottoman Turks invaded the Arabian peninsula and Qatar became part of Turkish rule within the region. The then Qasim Al-Thani, who had suceeded Mohammed, accepted Turkish rule while maintaining links with the British. In 1893 the Turks attacked Doha but were bravely repulsed by Qasim's forces. This further raised the stock of the Al-Thani and the process helped to unite the population of Qatar into a political and economic entity. An infrastructure of sorts began to appear and Qatar's freedom from Turkish influence laid the foundation for Qatar's independence of thought and action.

The Ottomans

By the First World War, the resurgent Wahhabis had reasserted themselves in the eastern part of Arabia. The Turks were thrown out, but by this time were fighting on the opposite side to the British. In 1916 Qasim's son Abdulla signed a Treaty by which the British guaranteed the safety of Qatar in return for Qatar's agreement not to deal with other foreign powers and not to engage in piracy or slave-trading.

World War I and II

By the 1930s, Ibn Saud, the leader of the Wahhabi Al-Sauds, was effectively ruling the entire Arabian peninsula. Although the rest of the Gulf States were not invaded, the political power and influence of Ibn Saud was enormous. Abdulla Al-Thani was always acutely aware of the threat on his doorstep and, when the promised protection from the British failed to materialise, he was obliged to pay off the Al-Saud to avoid direct invasion.

But a far more significant factor than the Al-Saud was about to appear, a force that would transform the whole region for all time. Oil. In 1932, oil was discovered in Bahrain and the concession was signed by a US consortium. Primitive though the oil geological surveys were, they suggested that the whole region might be immensely oil-rich. And they were right.

Oil

The British were quick to realise the potential of this black gold. Qatar had already given a British consortium, the Anglo Persian Oil Company (APOC), an oil concession, but they had chosen not to exploit it. The wise Abdullah used the concession to extract further defence guarantees. In 1935, a subsidiary of APOC – Petroleum Development Qatar Limited (PDL) – gained the rights to explore, and in 1939 oil began to flow from a well at Zakrit.

The Second World War interrupted production and development and even thereafter progress was sporadic. In 1963, the Qatar Petroleum Company was formed and concessions were awarded to a number of foreign operators, including Shell. Offshore production got under way in the mid-1960s and by 1976 the newly-formed state of Qatar took full State control of oil production, paving the way for the transformation of the country into the modern nation of today.

During the 1950s and 1960s, further impetus was given to the creation of a modern infrastructure. Roads, schools and hospitals sprang up. A power station was built. The Al-Thani dynasty passed the torch of leadership from generation to generation.

When the British announced their intention to pull out of the Gulf in treaty terms, considerable thought was given to how the smaller Gulf states might organise themselves. At one point, it seemed likely that Qatar and Bahrain would join Abu Dhabi, Dubai and the five northern Emirates to create a new federation of Arab Emirates. In the event, Qatar and Bahrain decided to strike out alone, with the other seven Emirates forming the United Arab Emirates (UAE) in 1971.

Independence

Qatar formulated a Constitution and declared its independence formally on 3 September 1971 – a date celebrated as National Day, an occasion for pride and reflection on achievement and ambition.

The following 20 years saw astonishing growth and development. Fuelled by ever increasing oil revenues, Qatar quickly acquired the trappings of a modern nation state. Social care grew in importance, and the welfare of Qatar's people became a major priority for the Government. Doha expanded rapidly, and the Qatari economy grew at an unprecedented rate. Vast numbers of expatriate workers – managerial and manual – had to be employed to ease the metamorphosis of crude oil into schools, shops, houses, a modern airport, a shipping port, telecommunications, hotels and all the trappings of First World infrastructure.

As Qatar began to grow up physically, so too did its political institutions. Keen to maintain its traditions of just and fair independent thinking, Qatar quickly joined the United Nations and the Arab League. It became a member of the International Monetary Fund and the World Bank. It has been a voice of calm and reason in all these bodies and has been an important element of the Gulf Cooperation Council (GCC).

In the 1990s, the development of the vast quantities of natural gas discovered in the waters off the north east coast further enhanced the nation's fortunes and prospects. Deposits in the North Dome field constitute the largest non-associated natural gas field in the world. Billions of dollars were raised to finance the exploitation of these resources and that investment is starting to pay off, with long-term off-take agreements guaranteeing a steady flow of cash into the nation's coffers.

The Political System

Qatar is governed by a monarchy. The Al-Thani family, as we have seen, has ruled the country since the 19th century. Power is transferred from the Ruler within the family usually, though not necessarily to a son.

The current Emir is Sheikh Hamad bin Khalifa Al-Thani; the Deputy Emir and Heir Apparent is Sheikh Jassim bin Hamad Al-Thani. The Prime Minister is Sheikh Abdullah bin Khalifa Al-Thani. There have been only two changes to the monarchy since the early 1970s – both by family consensus – underlining the stability of the regime.

The Emir is absolute Ruler and derives his power from the Constitution. He is bidden to rule according to principles of honesty, fairness, Islam, generosity and mutual respect. There is no government as the West understands the term and there are no political parties. The supreme legislative body is called the Advisory Council and is appointed by the Emir. It consists mainly of Ministers appointed by the Emir and acts as a rudder for development of laws and policy. The Ministers' more traditional role is to advise the Emir on issues in their areas of responsibility. The judicial system comes under the aegis of the Emir, though the vast majority of issues are settled by the application of Sharia (Islamic) law.

1

The Emir has pledged to push forward a programme of social and constitutional reform aimed at creating a progressive regime, a modern country, but one that stays true to historic and religious traditions and beliefs. As proof of this pledge the first ever municipal elections were held in March 1999, which enfranchised every Qatari citizen, male and female, over the age of 18. The elections were remarkable all the more for including women in the vote and permitting them to run for office. Several ladies did put their names forward, but none were returned.

In the same year the Emir established a committee with a mandate to study and draft a permanent constitution for the country within three years. That draft was completed and submitted to the Emir on 2 July 2002. It proposes that a 45-member Legislative Council, two-thirds of which would be elected by popular vote through a secret ballot and one-third by appointment, will sit for terms of four years. If adopted, the constitution will allow all nationals, over the age of 18 male and female, to vote and to stand for office. The draft also protects and guarantees freedom of speech, assembly, association, expression, opinion, scientific research and worship. These are indeed inspiring days for Qatar, which is once again lighting the way for its neighbours.

Qatar's history has been dramatic and turbulent, but the constants of sound rule, a clear spiritual philosophy and an independent streak will guard the safety and security of the nation.

Qatar in the 21st Century

Qatar today is a pleasant and self-assured country. Under the Emir, it enjoys governance which is supportive and socially responsible. Qatar continues to make the most of its greatest resources, oil, gas and its people.

The importance given to training and education is manifested in the development of schools and places of further education – all types of establishments from primary, preparatory and secondary school, to vocational, commercial and technical colleges. Specialised schools exist not only for those with handicaps and learning difficulties but also for the specially gifted. Yet others apply themselves to those with a leaning towards

1

the arts and theatre. Of course, in a Moslem country there is ample opportunity for the study and development of religious matters.

Work is underway to establish a new private university at the Qatar foundation, which will be affiliated with the best universities internationally.

Good health services in Qatar are available, from local clinics to major hospitals. New hospitals are being built and more doctors trained or recruited.

Qatar has had a vigorous National Theatre for many years – long before most of its neighbours had purpose-built theatres. There are thriving amateur dramatic and arts and crafts groups. From time to time there are first-class shows and arts displays from neighbouring regions and around the world. The National Library had its roots in one of the oldest libraries in the Gulf area and is well stocked and well patronised.

Qatari citizens have a real passion for sport. Being awarded the honour of hosting the Asian Games in 2006 is another catalyst to assist in developing the country's infrastructure and facilities.

Sport

Traditional sports also have their place in Qatar and continue to be heavily supported and pursued. These include dhow racing, which has its foundations in the seafaring, pearling and fishing livelihoods of the past. The sight of a fleet of dhows in full sail crewed by chanting men manhandling heavy canvas is really a sight to see. Falconry is more a popular pastime than competitive sport, and has reached new heights of interest among Qatari nationals in recent years. Camel racing is as popular as ever and new facilities have been built for all to enjoy. The racing of Arab horses, both endurance events across the desert flats and track racing, is also popular.

Among the modern sports, football comes first. However, the list of other popular sports to be found includes tennis, squash, table tennis, handball, basketball, sailing, scuba diving, motor rallying and swimming. Qatar has expressed the desire to become the Sports Capital of the Gulf and it stands a good chance of succeeding.

1

Women

While local women are generally fully covered in traditional dress, (including veil and mask), the outsider should not be drawn into believing they are a subjugated class. Their involvement and inclusion in every aspect of the community, business and even government is encouraged. The Emir's wife, Her Highness Sheikha Mouza plays an enormously important role in this encouragement. She has created an environment that encourages women to meet their social obligations and participate in public life. H.H. Sheikha Mouza also endorses women's conferences, which discuss and recommend solutions to the challenges confronting women who work outside the home. Her Highness has also been a leading light in developing various facilities for the education and encouragement of women to become actively involved in all aspects of modern life from education and banking to health, the arts and journalism, to the legal profession and Government.

Through this support there are now some Qatari ladies in positions of global importance. One of the more prominent and notable is H.E. Sheikha Dr. Ghalya Bint Mohammad Hamad Al-Thani, who was elected at the United Nations in New York to a four-year term as a member representing Qatar on the Committee on the Rights of the Child.

Not 10 years ago the West Bay was still salt flats and *subkha*. The first tower block had yet to be constructed. The grand gas projects were still in their infancy. The smart place to shop was still The Centre next to the Ramada. In less than a decade Qatar has been transformed.

Modernisation

Twenty-five and 30 storey buildings now tower over the Corniche around the Salam Towers (the first multi-storey buildings) and there are plans for another 100 buildings in the same area. West Bay has been filled and channels dredged to create a stylish living environment. The offshore wells, pipe lines, two major onshore gas plants of Qatargas and RasGas and their LNG (Liquefied Natural Gas) export terminals are up and running and earning revenue. The number of major shopping malls now runs into double figures and the old shopping centres have taken on a new lease of life.

The industrial townships of Messaieed, Dukhan and Ras Laffan are fast developing into vibrant communities with housing, shops, medical facilities and schools. Residential areas in and around the capital also sprout new housing compounds and villas by the score as old villas are torn down or remodelled.

The road improvement plan tries to keep pace with the increase in traffic. Inter-connecting secondary roads between the main roads are graded and covered with a hard tarmac running course in the place of dirt tracks; the familiar roundabouts are being replaced one by one by modern cross-roads with traffic lights and filter lanes. although they are still referred to as 'roundabouts'.

The old airport continues to be upgraded and improved, while the new airport is under construction. The single runway has the distinction of being one of the longest in the world.

There is an increasing amount to do when it comes to leisure time. There are more shops, more restaurants, more places to go and things to see. The development of a rash of new five-star hotels and resort complexes in recent times heralds a new era for the business and leisure visitor.

Qatar's streets remain substantially free from crime, and the expatriate community, which continues to make up the bulk of the population, goes about its business with little interference. The country has a modern and effective infrastructure, with improvements and further modernisation taking place all the time. Doha's hosting of the 2001 World Trade Organisation Summit Conference was another landmark moment in the country's determination to be a player on the world stage. The 2006 Asian Games (an event second in size and importance only to the Olympics), are also to be held in Qatar, giving further impetus to the development of the infrastructure.

The climate is harsh and hot for about one-third of the year – but made bearable by modern air-conditioning that allows year-round work and pleasure. Whilst Qatar is a Muslim country, and proudly so, it does not wear its beliefs aggressively. Tolerance and mutual respect allow freedom for citizens, residents and visitors alike.

Seen in the context of the region's history, modern Qatar has only been in existence for the blink of an eye. In that

1

short time it has become a mature and respected nation, and there is no better time for the businessman or tourist to get to know this fascinating country and its people.

1

2

investigating the
potential market

investigating the potential market

An outline of some of the myriad
organisations which exist to assist
the exporter, along with an
assessment of their focus and
likely relevance.

Before Arrival

The business traveller should, of course, be as well
informed as possible before entering a new market. This
section acts as a guide to where to find this information.
It includes government and private sources in electronic
and hardcopy format. The section also discusses the
availability of reliable market and economic information.

Whether you are visiting Qatar for the first time, or
making the latest in a series of regular visits, preparation
is essential if you are to get the most out of the trip and
ensure that your project succeeds. Obtaining the latest
information will allow you to plan effectively for your
visit, get a clear picture of the market you are entering,
identify any trends or opportunities that you can use to
your advantage and spot any possible pitfalls. It is
equally important to ensure that the information you use
is accurate and that you are aware of any possible bias.
The poor preparation of many business visitors is a
source of constant amazement to those working in
business support agencies. These days, there can be no
excuse for not knowing your facts. The resources are
plentiful, and in general people want to help. An hour's
research before you leave can save you a day in the
market.

The sources below provide a starting point for research
on the Qatar market. Many of them are free or provide
information at very little cost. However, much of this
information is not detailed enough for a thorough
appraisal of the market and will only give you an
overview.

Qatar is a small place with – outside the oil and gas
sectors – mostly niche business opportunities.
Accordingly, detailed formal business information on the
market is often limited. Qatar still operates largely on the
principles of word-of-mouth and personal contact. True
understanding comes only with visiting the country with
an open mind.

Qatari Embassies

Qatari Embassies in the UK and the USA are immensely
helpful in providing up-to-date information, as well as
pre-trip brochures and pamphlets about the country.
Contact details are as follows:

UK
1 South Audley Street
London
W1K 1NB
❏ Tel: +44 207 493 2200

USA
809 First Avenue 4th floor
NY 10017
❏ Tel: +12 12 486 9335

UK Ministries and other Government Agencies

In the UK, the primary British government source for information on overseas markets is British Trade International, which brings the export development and promotion resources of the Department of Trade and Industry and the Foreign and Commonwealth Office into one organisation. The brand name for its services is **Trade Partners UK** (TPUK). TPUK acts as a first point of contact for market and business information and it produces a suite of publications ranging from an introductory guide to the Gulf - the *Gulf Spotlight Yearbook* – to detailed sector analyses. It also offers specialist literature on agency law, etc. It offers a variety of services to small and medium-sized companies wanting to break into new markets, such as financial support for official trade missions and UK groups attending key exhibitions.

DTI

TPUK

2

The Qatar desk is at

Trade Partners UK
Kingsgate House
66-74 Victoria Street
London SW1E 6SW
❏ Tel: +44 207 215 4961; fax: +44 207 215 4831

Much of the above-mentioned information is available on Trade Partners UK's website at [www.tradepartners.gov.uk].

Through its Gateway Information Centre, Trade Partners UK provides information and advice direct to UK businesses. The Information Centre is a research facility available to exporters and their representatives wishing to undertake their own export market research. It provides access to a comprehensive collection of overseas market information – foreign economic and commercial statistics, trade and telephone directories (as publications, CD-ROMs or Internet databases), mail-order catalogues, information on the multilateral development agencies, including projects and initiatives which they are funding. Access is free. For further information, contact:

❑ Tel: +44 207 215 5444; fax: +44 207 215 4231
E-mail: [emic@xpd3.dti.gov.uk]

The **Export Market Information Research Service** (EMIRS) provides a fee-based research service based in the information centre for exporters and their representatives. These facilities are based at:

Kingsgate House
66-74 Victoria Street
London SW1E 6SW

Another source of assistance, which is totally free, is the **Trade Development Adviser** (previously called Export Promoters). In 1995, the then Secretary of State for Industry, Michael Heseltine, and his Minister for Trade, Richard Needham, launched an initiative to promote British exports. They proposed to second up to 100 people from British industry who were specialists either in certain countries or certain disciplines. These Trade Development Advisers (TDAs) are seconded to Trade Partners UK from British industry for a period of up to three years. The majority of these experts are businessmen with specialist knowledge of particular countries. In a few cases the promoter is an industry specialist, e.g. environment, power, etc. TDAs can be contacted by anyone. They are likely to be frequent visitors to their countries of responsibility and will have a lot of information relating to opportunities, agents, partners, exhibitions, trade missions, etc., but can generally be found through the Country Manager at Trade Partners in Kingsgate House. They often work from home. These TDAs are not only expected to be well informed but they are likely to be candid, and able to give direct answers about their markets and whether an opportunity for a particular company might exist. Their time and assistance is free and they will usually be able to help with introductions and contacts at the highest

2

level – they have a reporting line directly to the Minister for Trade in the UK. Overseas, they work closely with the Commercial Section of the Embassy.

Since Trade Development Advisers are, through the nature of their secondment, likely to change regularly, it is best to contact the Qatar desk at Kingsgate House to get the current contact details.

Another key feature of Trade Partners UK's support for the exporters, community is their website, a unique facility for finding new markets overseas. [www.TradeUK.com] is an Internet-based service designed to match British exporters with international opportunities. It is a free service provided by Trade Partners UK and operated by Applied Psychology Research (APR). It can be accessed by anyone, anywhere, at any time. [www.TradeUK.com] can help companies in two ways:

Firstly, they can register, free of charge, on the National Exporter's Database. This will make details of products and services available to overseas buyers free of charge. When companies register, their details are placed on the Internet, allowing overseas companies to find them through the database, which is widely advertised abroad. It is also possible to engineer a direct link to companies' own websites. Currently, over 55,000 companies are registered.

Secondly, companies can save time, money and effort gaining international sales leads through the Export Sales Leads Service, which offers hot business leads from the Trade Partners UK global network of staff based in the Commercial Sections of British Embassies and Consulates-General. These leads are matched to company requirements and e-mailed directly to them on the Internet. They include specific private sector opportunities; tenders and public sector opportunities; joint-venture and co-operation opportunities; and multilateral aid opportunities. In addition, market pointers showing trends around the world, plus direct entries from overseas companies, can be accessed. For further information go to [www.TradeUk.com] or contact:

❏ Tel: +44 207 925 7810; fax: +44 207 925 7770
E-mail: [export@smartlogic.com]

2

The Business Link network is a series of one-stop shops designed to meet local export and business requirements. All Business Links offer access to an Export Development Counsellor (EDC) who can assist with export related issues. For details of your nearest Business Link in England, contact:

❑ Tel: +44 345 567 765 or visit the Business Link Signpost website at [www.businesslink.co.uk]

Scotland: Scottish Trade International
❑ Tel: +44 9141-228 2812/2808
Website: [www.sti.org.uk]

Wales: Welsh Office Overseas Trade Services
❑ Tel: +44 1222 825 097
Website: [www.wales.gov.uk]

Northern Ireland: Industrial Development Board for Northern Ireland
❑ Tel: +353 2890 233233
Website: [www.idbni.co.uk]

Credit Guarantees

ECGD or the **Export Credits Guarantee Department** is a government department reporting to the Secretary of State for Trade and Industry. The ECGD exists primarily to insure export finance. Typically, a project is structured through the banking system, with ECGD providing a guarantee to the financing bank against default for commercial or political reasons.

ECGD

One of the most common ways in which ECGD becomes involved with an export is through a line of credit. When a UK bank offers a facility to an overseas bank to enable goods or services to be purchased from the UK, ECGD can insure that risk. The loan facility is used to pay the exporter once the goods have been exported or the service performed. If the borrower fails to repay any part of the loan then the UK bank is covered by the ECGD guarantee. Overseas investment insurance is also available, which offers protection for joint venture or equity investment abroad.

ECGD has played a pivotal role in the financing of Qatar's LNG (Liquefied Natural Gas) development and the team there is highly experienced in dealing major

2

deals in the market.

ECGD
PO Box 2200
2 Exchange Tower
Harbour Exchange Square
London E14 9GS
❑ Tel: +44 207 512 7000

There are a number of private sector companies which offer insurance against default on export contracts, e.g. NCM and Trade Indemnity.

Military Sales

Advice on military sales and equipment can be obtained from a specialist organisation in London, the **Defence Export Sales Organisation** (DESO), part of the Ministry of Defence. This is a very active export service manned by senior diplomats on temporary secondment to DESO. The business is, of course, highly specialised, and overseas is not handled by the embassy commercial offices but by the defence attachés. Defence sales include obvious military hardware and equipment, as well as the construction of airfields, supply of 4x4 vehicles and uniforms, etc. DESO will also advise on any relevant political sensitivities.

DESO
Ministry of Defence
Metropole Building
Northumberland Avenue, London WC2N 5BL
❑ Tel: +44 207 218 9000; fax: +44 207 807 8307

Other Ministries

The UK Department for Education and Skills takes no active part in promoting the export capabilities of its associated industries; this task is undertaken by the **British Council**. The Council is responsible for promoting British culture overseas and is very active in supporting UK educational and cultural enterprises. The Council, with offices across the UK, is financially self-supporting and is embracing the world of commerce with increasing vigour and imagination. It has officers responsible for exports and for liaison with other government bodies, in particular Trade Partners UK. The Council is very active in Qatar. Although still widely associated with its general promotion of British culture and the English language – and thus perhaps thought irrelevant to hardcore business – the Council is a leading proponent for the UK education and human resource development sector – an increasingly important sector in Qatar.

Contact details for the British Council in Qatar are:

The British Council
93 Al Sadd Street
PO Box 2992
Doha
Qatar
❏ Tel: +974 442 6193/4; fax: +974 442 3315
E-mail: [info@qa.britishcouncil.org]

The British Council in the UK can be contacted on,
❏ Tel: +44 207 389 4141 or at [www.britcoun.org] or [newweb.britcoun.org]

Two other ministries which promote British exports are the Department of Environment, Food and Rural Affairs (DEFRA) and The Department for Transport (DFT). Their export departments have specialised sector information freely available to all business people. Overseas visits by ministers and officials accompanied by business people are frequently arranged.

DEFRA: [www.maff.gov.uk]

DFT: [www.dft.gov.uk]

In general, all UK government offices can be found at [www.open.gov.uk] or in the excellent *Civil Service Yearbook* produced by the Cabinet Office and published by the Stationery Office, ❏ Tel: +44 870 600 5522.

The European Union

The most relevant office of the European Union (EU) is Directorate General 1 (DG1) which deals with trade and political matters; it is based in Brussels and has overseas representative offices. DG1 controls the Mediterranean Development Aid (MEDA) programme, a substantial sum for aid and loans (currently 11bn ecu) available for selected projects in the Middle East. DG1 also controls the **European Community Investment Partners** scheme (ECIP), finance for the region and relations with the **European Investment Bank** (EIB). DG1 has country desks, much the same as Trade Partners UK and the

EU

ECIP

FCO, with desk officers, who can offer information and assistance.

There are funds available from the Union for various development programmes apart from direct project finance, including money for companies to set up partnerships and/or joint ventures in the Middle East (though as the Gulf is relatively wealthy this rarely applies to Qatar). The ECIP scheme can assist with finance to form such a joint venture and for training of personnel. ECIP can also finance feasibility studies prior to a joint venture agreement.

Further assistance and advice can be obtained from various sources such as the Commercial Section of the United Kingdom Permanent Representation (UKRep) office in Brussels, which exists to assist British companies to understand and participate in the programmes administered by the European Institutions in Brussels. The Arab British Chamber of Commerce in London can also offer advice on the labyrinth that is Brussels. Registration with Brussels is essential for consultants. Manufacturers with specialised products should also pre-qualify to participate in EU-funded projects.

US

The US State Department and the Department of Commerce provide a wide range of information to US companies or representatives of US companies operating in Qatar. This includes the *Country Commercial Guide*, which is a comprehensive coverage of the business environment in Qatar. This is naturally written with US business in mind, but much of the information is more generally applicable. The *Country Commercial Guides* can be downloaded from the Internet at: [www.state.gov/www/about_state/business/com_guides/index.html].

Canada

The Department of Foreign Affairs and International Trade is actively involved in Qatari affairs, and participated in organising the World Trade Organization in Doha in 2001. The Department can be contacted at:

Lester B. Pearson Building
125 Sussex Drive
Ottawa, Ontario
K1A 0G2
❏ Fax: +1 (613) 944-7981

Further Sources of Information

The following list of bodies is not definitive, but indicates the types of organisations that exist and how they might help.

The Middle East Association

The Middle East Association is an independent private organisation set up in 1961 by a number of British companies to promote trade between the UK and the Middle East. It is a non-political and non-profit making organisation financed entirely by private subscription. It works closely with Middle Eastern Embassies in London and with other official and semi-official bodies such as the FCO, Trade Partners UK, the ECGD, and the Confederation of British Industry (CBI). It also liaises with other trade associations and Chambers of Commerce and Industry in the UK and overseas. The aim of the Association is to offer its members advice on all aspects of Middle East trade and to channel to them business opportunities, introductions and enquiries from overseas. The Association has a library and information centre at its offices in Bury Street. With the support of Trade Partners UK, it sponsors overseas missions and UK participation in trade exhibitions in the Middle East. The Association holds regular functions at its headquarters for its members, which include lunches with guest speakers from the Middle East. A fortnightly information digest is circulated to its members. People with a long and deep experience of the Arab world populate the MEA's executive and board. Joining the Association is an excellent way of gaining access to the Gulf 'loop' in the UK – and the MEA is responsible for organising the British half of the heroically named QBAB – the Qatar British Association of Businessmen.

MEA

MEA

Bury House
33 Bury Street, St James's
London SW1Y 6AX
❏ Tel: +44 207 839 2137; fax: +44 207 839 6121;
website: [www.the-mea.co.uk]
E-mail: [mail@the-mea.co.uk]

Arab British Chamber of Commerce

The Arab British Chamber of Commerce (ABCC) was set up in 1975 and represents all the Arab Chambers of

2

ABCC

Commerce and the main UK Chambers. The ABCC is responsible for mutual trade and economic interests through meetings, exhibitions and publications throughout the Middle East, with the exception of Egypt. A regular journal is freely available to those interested. The ABCC is also a facilitator for the European Community Investment Partners scheme (ECIP) and has details of how to access the programme, together with details of many of the other EU funding programmes. The ABCC has a team of specialists dealing with documentation and legal issues and are unfailingly helpful.

ABCC
Belgrave Square
London SW1X 8PH
❑ Tel: +44 207 235 4363; fax: +44 207 245 6688
E-mail: [bims@abccbims.force9.co.uk]

Chambers of Commerce or any trade or professional body that you belong to may be able to provide information on Qatar. They may not produce the material themselves but as a member you may have access to their library where such information is held. These bodies may also conduct research on your behalf for a fee. This is a more costly method but can save time. You should be very specific in defining your research project to obtain the maximum benefit.

Qatar British Business Forum

QBBF

There is an extremely active local community of professional British and Qatari businessmen within The Qatar British Business Forum (QBBF). Their objective is to use their business knowledge and connections to promote Qatari-British business relations and to offer a link for British Trade Missions and UK organisations promoting Middle East/UK trade. The QBBF consults with the British Embassy in Doha on matters of joint interest and assists the Embassy by providing contacts and support to Inward Trade Missions, prominent businessmen and officials visiting Qatar from the United Kingdom, all with a view to promoting bilateral economic relations. Contact the QBBF via the Embassy, or directly by email at [qbbf@qatar.net.qa] or their website [www.qbbf.com], which has a wealth of information and contact details of the 100+ local companies who are members.

The Web

Search engines will of course lead to several of the many websites displaying information on Qatar. Below are a few direct sites that I have found to be useful and up-to-date:

[www.arab.net]

[www.qatar-info.com]

[www.cia.gov] (Search for Qatar)

[www.emulateme.com/qatar]

[www.travel.state.gov/qatar]

[www.mofa.gov.qa]

Digging Deeper

Once you have gained an overview of the market in Qatar, you may want more detailed economic information or wish to concentrate on your particular sector. This is where the cost of research starts to increase – but you will be very well informed and the risk of unpleasant surprises later on will be much reduced. You will be aware of the trends and the possible effects on your business and therefore able to plan for them.

Economic and Country Guides

There are a multitude of resources available. Generally, banks (particularly large international banks), will be a useful source of information, and can usually be accessed through their websites. Also worth bearing in mind are the trade associations – there is one for almost every conceivable industry in the UK. Some of these are large and can be very active in promoting exports. These organisations will assist their members to take part in trade fairs, can organise seminars and conferences to run concurrently with these events and may target particular countries where they believe the greatest opportunities exist for their members.

Full lists of all the associations in the UK are available from CBD Research Ltd in Kent, who publish a directory in hard copy or in CD-ROM format – full details at [www.glen.co.uk]. Further information is also available from Trade Partners UK.

2

Trade Associations

Seminars and conferences are a good place to meet others associated with Qatar or with a particular industry – oil and gas, in the case of Qatar. The content of the presentations at such gatherings and the opportunities for networking during the intervals are both important. The Middle East Association (see above) holds a monthly 'at home' where members meet and discuss the different issues and opportunities in the area, including Qatar.

A few specific suggestions are as follows:

Dun & Bradstreet (D&B)

D&B offer an authoritative web-based information service that includes data on Qatar. The D&B Country Risk Service provides comprehensive information for evaluating risk and opportunities. The approach is to combine constant monitoring with an archive service on a wide range of topics. Most companies can qualify for a 14-day free trial period. D&B also offer two excellent business support publications. The first is *The Exporters' Encyclopaedia* – an annual publication that provides information and advice on exporting to almost every country in the world. The second is the *International Risk and Payment Review* – a monthly publication that allows companies to keep up-to-date on issues affecting the global trading environment.

D&B can be contacted at:

Holmer's Farm Way
High Wycombe
Bucks
HP12 4UL
❑ Tel: +44 1494 422000; fax: + 44 1494 422260;
Website: [www.dunandbrad.co.uk]

or

Dun and Bradstreet
899 Eaton Avenue
Bethlehem
PA 18025

USA
❑ Tel: +1 8009 32 0025; fax: +1 610 882 6005

Economist Intelligence Unit (EIU)
The Economist Intelligence Unit produces a range of quarterly and annual publications, which provide a

detailed political and economic analysis of Qatar. They offer a *Country Report*, which is an up-to-date monitoring information service, a *Country Profile*, which combines historical data and background with current reportage plus a forecast service called the *Country Risk Service*.

EIU

The EIU can be contacted at:
15 Regent Street
London
SW1Y 4LR
❏ Tel: +44 207 830 1000; fax: +44 207 830 1023
E-mail: london@eiu.com
website: [www.eiu.com]

Or

The Economist Building
111 West 57th Street
New York, NY 10019, USA
❏ Tel: +1 212 554 0600; fax: +1 212 586 1181

Middle East Economic Digest
Another valuable source of information is MEED (Middle East Economic Digest) who publish a number of country reports and financial profiles, including the *Middle East Business Finance Directory* of the top 500 companies in the region. MEED also offers a CD-ROM offering archive material going back five years. The *Middle East Economic Digest* itself, though perhaps a slightly dry read, is, nonetheless, mandatory reading for anyone who wants to keep abreast of commercial, economic and political issues in the region. MEED has a first-class team of writers based in the region and developments in Qatar are regularly and thoroughly reported.

MEED
21 John Street
London WC1N 2BP
❏ Tel: +44 207 505 8000; fax: +44 207 831 9537
Website: [www.meed.com]

Reuters Business Briefing
Information and news/archive material can be found from Reuters Business Briefing a CD-ROM or web-based information service, allowing subscribers to search a vast range of information sources for material on virtually any

2

subject matter. It is particularly good at digesting and reproducing news from the Middle East and is a good way of following trends as well as tracking down information on individual companies.

Dow Jones Reuters Business Briefing
Reuters Limited
85 Fleet Street
London
EC4P 4AJ
❑ Tel: + 44 207 542 5043

Travel Advice

Information about flights, visas and the like is contained in Chapter 3. This section deals with such matters as health concerns and security issues – of which there are none of real consequence in Qatar.

The most convenient source of travel advice from the UK is the Foreign and Commonwealth Office (FCO) Travel Advisory Service. This can be accessed free either by telephone or on-line. It provides succinct information and advice on natural disasters, health concerns, security and political issues. It is more than adequate for most business travellers' needs. Be aware though that it is aimed at a wide audience and is not geared solely towards the business visitor's requirements.

The FCO travel advisory service can be contacted on:

❑ Tel: +44 207 238 4503/4
Website: [www.fco.gov.uk/travel]

The US State Department Advice Service can be found at:

Website: [www.state.gov/travel_warnings.html]

Their reports can sometimes seem alarmist, as the US State Department is legally obliged to publish any threats to US citizens and their property of which it is aware. Also see [www.usis.egnet.net].

For travel information and advice geared specifically towards the business travellers' needs, you must turn to the private sector. Here there are some good but expensive services that provide more frequently updated reports than the FCO or State Department travel notices. These services tend to be more forward looking, commenting for instance on the likelihood of further security incidents or the possible deterioration or improvement in the travel environment. They are also usually more frank about a country as they do not have the political restrictions under which the FCO or State Department must operate. But the stability of Qatar – notwithstanding the nature of some of its near(ish) neighbours – makes this service practically unnecessary.

Keeping Up-to-Date

Publications

After you have thoroughly researched the Qatar market and started operations in the country, it is essential to keep up-to-date about developments both in your particular sector and in the wider market.

The easiest method to achieve this is to monitor the press and media for stories on Qatar. The country receives adequate coverage in the international press and most British newspapers and news organisations have correspondents based in the region. The Internet editions of some newspapers and media organisations offer news e-mail services, which send you stories on specified subjects to your e-mail address. Others allow you to produce customised pages, which are updated with stories on your chosen subjects. One of the best is CNN's service, on [www.cnn.com].

There are three magazines that offer good and slightly offbeat insights into the commercial world of Qatar and the Gulf.

The first is *Gulf Business* – a glossy and informative look at the commercial and economic scene published monthly by Motivate Publishing in Dubai. Motivate launched a 'Qatar Edition' of *Gulf Business* in July 2002.

❑ Tel: +971 (0)4 282 4060; fax: +971 (0)4 282 4436
E-mail: [motivate@emirates.net.ae]
Website: [www.gulfbusiness.com]

The second is *Gulf Marketing Review* which, as its title suggests, concentrates on marketing issues in the Gulf – a rather neglected field apart from this worthy monthly publication. Full of news on trends and ideas, it gives a clear picture of the advertising, marketing and PR scene which is developing apace in the region and is surfacing in Qatar.

2

❑ Tel: +971 (0)4 349 6663; fax: +971 (0)4 349 9552
E-mail: [info@gmr-online.com]
Website: [www.gmr-online.com]

Thirdly, the quarterly magazine *Forum*, sponsored by the Qatar British Business Forum, The British Embassy Commercial Section and The British Council. This publication evolved from the QBBFs newsletter and is packed with solid updated information on matters of direct interest to companies in both countries wishing to do business with each other. More information is available through the Embassy, the British Council, the QBBF or by direct contact with the compiler dch Interim Management.

❑ Tel: and fax: +974 4682549
E-mail: [chaddock@qatar.net.qa]
Website: [www.dchonline.org]

Croner is a leading publisher of loose-leaf, regularly updated guidance on international trade. Their comprehensive Reference Book for Exporters concentrates on the practicalities of import and export procedures for over 170 countries, and explains both UK and foreign government regulations and restrictions in detail. In addition, Croner's website, [tradeinternational-centre.net], is a good place to find free Country information, and register for free e-newsletters on your areas of interest. 2002 also saw the re-launch of a monthly subscription magazine *Trade International Digest*.

Croner
145 London Road
Kingston upon Thames
Surrey
KT2 6SR
❑ Tel: +44 20 8547 3333, fax: +44 20 8547 2638
Website: [www.tradeinternational-centre.net]

2

getting to Qatar

3

getting to Qatar

Various considerations in
arranging travel to Qatar

Before examining the practicalities of travel, it is important to get some paperwork done. Unless you are a citizen of the Gulf Cooperation Council, you will need a visa in order to enter Qatar. That applies to all visitors to Qatar, be they businessmen or tourists. However, the rules have changed in the last few years and continue to do so with the desire of Qatar to become an up-market tourist destination.

In the 1970s visas were not required for British citizens who found that entry was a relatively simple matter of showing the old blue, hard covered, book passport. That situation (as far as Qatar was concerned) continued until the EU decided in the mid-1990s that Britain must make all Gulf State nationals apply for a visa to enter Britain. In response, British passport holders suddenly found themselves needing a visa for Qatar.

However, the process was made easy by the fast turn around of visas at the Qatari Embassy in London, and multiple entry visas being made available to British and American nationals. The speed of service in fact prevented one visitor to Qatar's Embassy in London from obtaining a multiple entry visa the first time. Having just submitted his application for a single entry visa he discovered that multi-entry visas existed and immediately requested a change to his application. Unfortunately, his first application had already been processed and stamped in his passport and could not be changed. (Note: Such speed of service should not be expected in Qatar.)

A prerequisite of a successful visa application is to have a sponsor. But this is not as daunting as it might sound. Although a sponsor is effectively there to guarantee your conduct and be responsible for you during your stay, the sponsor can actually be your hotel – and for the majority of business visitors, this is the preferred route. Not so good if you are to stay with friends or relatives, because the hotel does expect the visitor to stay with them for at least the first night. Other sponsors can be Qatari nationals, Qatar-registered companies or the salaried head of a household, including resident expatriates with a valid residence permit, who can sponsor dependants, which includes servants.

3

One of the recent, user friendly, changes is that GCC residents do not need to have a visa stamped in their passport prior to travel since they can obtain one at the airport on arrival. Others given the same dispensation are visitors with British, American and some other passports (see below) who are arriving via Qatar Airways. However, this can be a lengthy process depending what other flights arrive with yours and, sometimes, the mood of the immigration officials. The best advice is, if possible, to get a visa stamped in your passport prior to travel – it just avoids one more potential hassle.

A final guideline in this preamble is to check with the local Qatari Embassy. As noted above, the rules are changed frequently and the understanding, interpretation and implementation of the current rules, particularly by busy airline counter staff when you are checking in for a flight, is what can best be described as variable.

3

Qatar Airways:

Since the arrival of Chief Executive Officer Akbar Al Baker in 1996, Qatar Airways has undergone a reshaping of large proportions. Once a small regional airline serving only the Gulf, this airline has grown in customer service, infrastructure and size to exist now as an important carrier to Europe and the Far East.

Not perhaps of foremost interest to the business traveller, but useful to know of for potential clients, Qatar Airways now boasts Qatar Airways Holidays, offering tourists package holidays at special prices. Only two years old, this branch of Qatar Airways is making use of the country's growing tourism industry and natural resources to attract people to its benefits.

Visas

Since December 2001, Qatar has been able to offer a straightforward tourist or business 14-day extendable visa for a mere QR55 to passengers (Qatar Airways) simply on arrival at Doha International Airport for passports holders from the following 33 countries:

USA, UK, France, Italy, Germany, Canada, Australia, New Zealand, Japan, The Netherlands, Belgium,

Luxemburg, Switzerland, Austria, Sweden, Norway, Denmark, Portugal, Ireland, Greece, Finland, Spain, Monaco, Vatican, Iceland, Andorra, San Marino, Liechtenstein, Brunei, Singapore, Malaysia, Hong Kong, South Korea.

If you are not from one of the countries listed above, you can apply for visas in the following ways:

Business Visa
These are the norm – believe it or not – for business visitors. They are valid for seven days (though extendable for up to a month) and can be processed in a day or two. The visa will be valid from the date of issue for three months and must be used within that time. The sponsors will present the visa form at the airport and send a copy to you. When you arrive, your copy is matched to the original and your passport stamped. Such visas can be arranged through Qatari Embassies overseas, but the hotel/sponsor route is probably simpler.

Tourist Visa
The Tourist Visa is valid for up to 28 days and may be obtained upon application to one of the major hotels. These are obtainable by hotels for guests who will be staying at the hotel throughout their visit. They are limited to that booking and require proof of a return ticket in order to be issued. They cannot be extended. Your local travel agent should be able to sort all this out for you.

Visitor's Visa
British passport holders with the right of abode in Britain may obtain a Visitor's Visa for up to six months on application to the Qatari Embassy in London, or other Qatari Embassies outside England.

Multiple Entry Visas
It is also possible to obtain Multiple Entry Visas if you are a British or American passport holder. British citizens can obtain the visa valid for up to 5 years, depending on the validity of the passport, whereas Americans can obtain the document with validity up to 10 years. The visa is valid for both business and tourist purposes with a maximum length of stay of six months, after which the holder must leave the country.

3

Residence and Work Visit Visas

A Residence Visa is valid for up to three years and is granted to those with employment contracts to work in Qatar. The person is invariably sponsored through the company with which they have the employment contract. With this visa the individual can bring their families (under their own sponsorship) and get an official ID number, health card, driving licence and all the trappings of living in the country full time. The Work Visit Visa was introduced in February 2000 and allows residence of up to one year and is renewable on a yearly basis.

Driving Licence

Visitors may drive a rented car on their UK, American and most other European licences for a week, but for longer periods they will need to obtain a temporary Qatari Licence. Their car-hire company usually quickly arranges this for them. Residents must have a valid full Qatari Driving Licence, which is obtained only after the residence permit is obtained.

Travelling to Qatar

Having got your visa or satisfied yourself that a visa can be obtained, you will need to think about how to get to Qatar. Entry points into Qatar may be made by land through the main border point at Abu Samra, on the boarder with Saudi Arabia, by air through Doha International Airport or by sea through the ports of Doha and Messaieed.

Travelling to Qatar overland by car from the UAE or Bahrain is not particularly long or arduous. It is a pleasant alternative way for the business traveller to occupy the dead time of the weekend. Sadly, at the time of writing such a jaunt would entail entering and leaving Saudi Arabia, with all the additional visa paperwork and lost time at the borders (yes plural), so it is not really practical. However, there will be considerably more overland travel once the causeway with Bahrain is operational. There have also been several attempts in recent years to have regular sea ferry services between Qatar and its neighbours. But these are for the future and as most readers of this guide will fly in and out, leaving other routes to intrepid tourists, the emphasis here is on flying.

The local and European airlines that serve Qatar with direct flights from European starting points are Qatar Airways, British Airways and KLM.

British Airways and Qatar Airways offer a daily direct service whilst KLM fly four times a week to Amsterdam, (Schipol). All three also provide more flights with local (Dubai, Abu Dhabi or Bahrain) connections but for the most part these will be on the same plane, so there is no hassle about having to get off and losing your bags a few kilometres up the Gulf. Of course, you have the opportunity to travel on another favoured world-class airline, if you want to hop via Bahrain or Dubai, but this will mean a change of plane and additional hours on your flying time which is fine if you are an airport shop-a-holic.

Schedules being what they are, there is no point in explaining the current (Summer 2002) availability of flights. The best advice is to consult the airlines directly to find out what best fits your needs. It is so easy these days on the Internet to make bookings.

British Airways: [www.britishairways.com]

Qatar Airways: [www.qatarirways.com]

KLM: [www.klm.com]

The Middle East and Europe being where (and what) they are means that the majority of flights are overnight trips. Europe restricts air transport between midnight and 0600, and many flights are enroute to or from the Far East. The Middle East perforce becomes a night-time starting point or destination. This is not a problem for Qatar since, like most of its neighbours, it is pretty much a night-time place anyway. Try getting out of the traffic jam and into the supermarket at midnight!

If travelling at night is something you really want to avoid, all airlines have options for day flights. The most frequent is Qatar Airways, followed by British Airways. Your choice of carrier will probably be dictated by schedules. But for local flavour, the vote goes to Qatar Airways (they serve alcohol 'wet' unlike most Arab-based carriers). If you want to drop in to Bahrain for some good duty-free shopping, then Gulf Air is a good option, as is Emirates Air if you want to try Dubai's new and immense airport facilities. Mind you, Qatar's Doha airport has had, and is continuing with, a major facelift with enormously improved facilities and shopping for departing passengers. This will get even better with the construction of the new airport terminals now in progress.

3

On arrival

Qatar is a Moslem country and has rules about what is and is not permissible to bring into the country. In short, don't even think about drugs or other narcotics (that goes for anywhere), alcohol, pork or pork products, non-Moslem religious items, or any materials which may be considered pornographic and that includes many magazines commonly found in bookstores in the West. Be prepared to have videos confiscated for inspection. You will be given a receipt and they will be returned if found acceptable.

Trade Missions

Another route to get into the country is with a trade mission. For the first-time traveller in particular, these offer a soft entry to the market, accompanied by a mission leader experienced in both business and travel. The organisers will help the visitor deal with all the minutiae of pre-travel documents and travel arrangements and the mission leader and no doubt one or two other old hands will assist if things become a bit confusing.

These ventures are usually arranged with the local support of both the Embassy and appropriate Business Groups formed from the resident business community. Once in the country the missionaires tend to have a fairly strong series of briefings and meetings with as wide a cross section of organisations as their limited time will allow. Great for an overview or to get a feel, but again, please do your own homework first!

Health and Insurance

By and large Qatar is a healthy and safe place to be. Medical, dental and hospital care in Qatar is of a high standard. The Government-owned Hamad Medical Centre is the primary hospital and has an excellent reputation in dealing with trauma and heart conditions. Other private clinics and hospitals are being introduced and the standard is likely to be equally high.

Whilst the visitor will not go untreated for lack of a health card or cash in Qatar, it is sensible to ensure that you are covered for all medical eventualities, including repatriation. If you are employed, your company should

3

ensure that you have proper cover. If not, there are many companies providing this service, such as BUPA, ExpaCare, IHI and PPP, which can be checked out via the web.

Bupa International: [www.bupa-intl.com]

ExpaCare: [www.expacare.net]

IHI: [www.ihi.dk]

PPP: [www.ppphealthcare.com]

3

the ground rules

4

the ground rules

This section takes the reader by
the hand and talks through the
nitty-gritty of everyday life,
from how to get around to how
much to tip the bell-boy.

Money

The currency of Qatar is the Qatar Riyal (QR) which is
divided into 100 Dirhams (not to be confused with the
UAE Dirham, which has almost the same value as a
Qatari Riyal). Coins are available in 1, 5, 25, 50 Dirham
(or *Halalas*), although one seldom sees the smallest two
in circulation. Notes are issued for 1, 5, 10, 50, 100 and
500 Riyals. At the time of writing, the Qatari Riyal was
trading at around 5.45 to the Pound Sterling, 3.53 to the
Euro and essentially fixed to the United States Dollar at
3.64. Currency is freely convertible and there are any
number of ways to bring it in and send it out of the
country – more of which later.

Banks

Top of the list is the Qatar Central Bank (QCB), the
Government bank, which was established by Royal
Decree in 1985 and is the regulator and controller of all
other banks. Don't expect to waltz into the QCB to open
an account since retail and commercial banking is not
their thing.

The banking sector is comprised of 15 banks. Of these,
five are commercial banks, two are Islamic banks, two
are (non-Qatari) Arab, five are foreign and one is
government-owned, the Qatar Industrial Development
Bank. There are more than 100 branches in the country
and the numbers are constantly growing, with a
particular emphasis on reaching the developing outer
reaches of the country in the industrial cities to the
south, north and west of the capital.

Personal Finances
Banks
The financial sector in Qatar is relatively sophisticated.
Armed with a supply of traveller's cheques (US Dollar
cheques are best, but most major currencies will be fine)
and your plastic, you will survive and prosper.
Obviously, for everyday transactions, particularly in
small stores, supermarkets and *suqs*, cash is still king – as
a rule, the more air-conditioned your surroundings, the
better the odds are of being able to use plastic. Forget
cheques – some retail outlets even refuse to accept
cheques drawn from local banks.

4

All the main banks have ATM facilities, and more are installed every day. These holes-in-the-wall are linked to your own domestic systems and will accept a wide range of cards such as Visa, Cirrus, Plus, MasterCard and NAPS.

A word of warning: if you are intent on using these ATMs, make sure you understand the charges that your own bank will levy in different circumstances. Shopping is easy as most outlets accept debit cards (called the NAPS system in Qatar). You will have to get used to having others crowding around and watching you openly enter your 'secret' PIN number.

If you are planning to become resident in Qatar, it is recommended that you open a bank account. This is a relatively straightforward process – assuming you earn enough money (the banks have different rules on how much you have to earn before they'll accept you as a customer). Shop around for the best deals, as the banking sector is becoming increasingly competitive as the economy matures. Home banking and payment of utility and other bills, via a direct connection or through the Internet, is the norm in Qatar with almost all local bank accounts.

4

Following the lead of the oil and gas industry, the banks have changed their core working hours and days to 0730 to 1300 Sunday to Thursday. Banks are closed on Fridays and Saturdays. There are some other modifications like late-night working and extended hours in certain locations where the standard hours would be inconvenient. You will also find that banks are open at different times during the holy month of Ramadan. But the ATMs work 24 hours a day (unless they actually run out of the stuff which has been known to happen during public holidays).

Exchange Houses

As noted above, exchange houses independent from the banks exist to change money and send remittances. These are not like the kiosks in major cities and other tourist destinations in the West. They offer an excellent service to the expatriates and migrant workers to remit home, and offer competitive rates and charges often beating those of the banks. Don't assume the bank will give you the best deal and don't assume that all rates will be the same. If you have the time, shop around until you feel comfortable with the rate and charges being offered.

Transport

There is no bus service, no trains, no metro, and no tram in Qatar. If you want to get around, you are left with either self-propulsion (foot, bike, hire car or motorcycle) or a choice between a limousine service (known elsewhere as a minicab) or the orange-and-white city taxis, which appear to be engaged in some kind of fast breeding programme.

Useful facts about the country:	
Capital	Doha
Population	600,000
Area	11,437 sq. km.
Official Language	Arabic
Official Religion	Islam
Currency	Qatari Riyal (QR)
Time Zone	GMT + 3
Climate	Winter 20-30°c
	Summer 25-48°c
IDD Code	+ 974
Transportation	Taxis/car rental
Business Hours:	
Offices and Shops	0800-1200 hrs
	1600-1900 hrs
Shopping Malls	0900-2200 hrs
Weekend	Thursday afternoon/Friday

4

Taxis

The taxis are one of the joys of Doha. A law unto themselves, they belt around the capital, hooting and honking, more on the lookout for business than other vehicles or pedestrians. They will stop pretty much anywhere to pick up a fare, so don't worry about finding a suitable spot to stand. In fact, if you stand still in Doha for more than a few seconds, a ton of orange and white metal will come looking for you.

Taxis are very cheap and are metered, which saves haggling. Haggling is all very well, and you might shave a *Halala* or two off the price, but if you don't really know where you're going, the meter is a comfort. And as you will struggle to spend over QR10 for a trip around town, don't worry about it.

Taxi drivers on the whole know the city like the back of their hands. Their command of English varies, but they will get you there in the end. The condition of their vehicles ranges from not very good to a lot worse but you can bet your bottom *Halala* that the radio works. And if your idea of fun is zooming down the Corniche with the windows down, engine roaring, local pop music blaring, then the Doha taxi experience is for you.

Limousines

Some people just will not lower themselves to loiter on the street-side to hail and ride in a taxi. It really is not everyone's cup of tea and anyway when you are going nicely dressed in a dinner jacket or ball gown to a swank do at the Ritz Carlton, pitching up in a taxi is not quite the thing. At some times of day actually finding a taxi can be difficult. Taxis are particularly hard to find in the early morning and lunchtime because they are widely used (on contract) by families to ferry children to and from school.

A more sedate (and more comfortable) alternative is the limousine. These are smart cars (Lexus and Jaguar from the two main operators), with uniformed chauffeurs, air-conditioning, etc. They must be booked in advance (your hotel will do this for you) and are perhaps more suitable for longer trips and late night journeys to and from your place of residence. They cost three or four times the going rate for regular taxis, but several times not-very-much is still rather cheap.

At the Airport

Arriving at the airport can be fraught, especially if you are arriving for the first time and are not being met. All hotels have a meet and assist service. Ensure that your hotel knows you want collecting on arrival and they will be there with sign board waiting as you walk out of customs. Some even have a chap floating around inside immigration to make sure you are there and that you know they are too.

If you don't have hotel transport laid on, again you have the choice of taxis or limousines, both of which will be ready to assist. For a taxi, you need to walk outside the building to the taxi rank. The limo drivers tend to hover inside looking for lost souls who needs transport.

As for cost, airport taxis, as is the tradition everywhere, take a different approach to their counterparts plying the streets of the capital. In their view, the journey from the airport to anywhere is QR20-30 and they don't run meters. You have a number of choices; pay, haggle and run the risk of losing the ride, or stagger/walk/crawl/jog to the nearest public highway and hail a passing cab. The limo service from the airport is, at QR30-50, not much more expensive – and the driver will have a sheet of charges to the common destinations.

Car Rental

Renting a car is an option for the short stay as well as the longer-term visitor, neither of whom should be of a nervous disposition. A wide range of rental vehicles is available and you can drive on your national licence for seven days. Thereafter, you need to apply for a temporary or permanent Qatari licence. The rental companies are well versed in the procedures and will help you with the paperwork and talk you through the test, which involves some testing of eyesight as well as driving skills. Driving in Qatar can be, quite literally, a hit and miss affair and it may be better to leave the steering wheel in the hands of local experts. If you are driving and are involved in an accident, the golden rule is to stay with your vehicle, no matter where it is. The police will come to the scene and prepare their report. Without that, you – and your car – will not go anywhere. It almost goes without saying that Qatar has extremely cheap petrol (gasoline). Car theft is practically unknown, as is theft from cars. If you leave you car unlocked with your briefcase crammed with papers and money lying on the back seat, the chances are that it will all be there when you return. On the other hand, you wouldn't do that at home so why run the risk in Qatar? This is still the real world, so be sensible.

Communications

Telephone and Internet

What did people in Qatar do before the telephone? It's hard to imagine, because Qataris and foreigners alike seem to be constantly on the phone, and the arrival of mobile phones has made matters 10 times worse. You get the impression, on passing through immigration at Doha International Airport, that you are handed a cell phone, which is then clamped to your ear for you to shout into for the duration of your visit.

The phone system in Qatar is as efficient as anywhere. Landlines are good and the GSM system works very well. Calls within Qatar by landline are free. It is easy to buy or rent mobiles in Doha; and prepaid SIM cards are available from QTel, the local (in fact the only, since it's a monopoly) telecommunications company. They also run the cable TV system and the Internet. QTel comes in for a lot of criticism for high-handedness, high prices and poor service; however, the company has been making efforts since being privatised to address these matters which primarily affect resident users rather than visitors.

The Internet is becoming increasingly popular in Qatar with private use growing at a speed that is putting a strain on QTel's ISP capacity, particularly at peak times. There are a growing number of Internet cafés in Doha that run on faster, leased, lines.

Here is a list of a few of these increasingly popular institutions:

Al Bida Internet Café	❑ Tel: 435 0070
Gulf Internet Café	❑ Tel: 435 0060
Granada Internet Café	❑ Tel: 488 8817
Qatar Internet Café	❑ Tel: 435 0711

Dialing Codes

The usual international dialing codes apply, with the exception that the exit code for Qatar is '0'. (Trying to explain to the person who is having trouble getting an international line that the code isn't 'two zero's', but that one should only dial 'one zero', causes confusion. Perhaps saying 'use a single zero instead of two' would be clearer but seldom is the longer phrase the first thought!)

Mail and Courier

Currently, mail is not delivered to homes or offices. All mail is collected from Post Office Boxes. There was some movement to start delivery to major concerns, but since this means the very top echelon of the government and quasi-government sector, it will hardly affect the average visitor. Various forms of transmittal service are available from ordinary overland envelope mail through airmail,

4

parcel and registered services and even into a form of local courier service by the name 'Mumtaz Post'. (*Mumtaz* means 'excellent' in Arabic, which by and large is an apt description of the service provided). The public mail service does work and in some parts very efficiently, whilst in others less so. As an example, regular airmail from England can take as little as 24 hours or more than a week to arrive in the mailbox. It seems to depend rather on the time of year and local holidays. Local mail is not very efficient, and most people don't rely on this if time is of the essence. Most international courier companies have a presence in Qatar, but the Post Office has a monopoly on all internal mail, and at the present time allows no private courier service to carry mail within the country.

Television and Radio

The advent of satellite TV has transformed the lot of the hotel-based business traveller. It was not so long ago that flicking through the channels during the afternoon lull or before turning in would produce a choice between readings from the Holy Qur'an, interminable Egyptian soap-operas or a film. All these fine viewing options are still available, but most hotels now also feature a wide range of satellite channels too. That is not to say that the programmes on offer are of much higher quality – the stations seem to buy American drama series by the mile – but nowadays there is a much greater choice of rubbish.

Satellite apart, the local TV station, QTV, has two channels. QTV Channel One is the Arabic channel (where all programmes are in Arabic, except late night English movies which are subtitled in Arabic). The other is QTV Channel Two, which continues to be billed as 'Your Entertainment Channel'. It has a good mixture of programmes mostly in English, but does have a tendency to put local sport (with Arabic commentary) in the place of those advertised. However, they do show late night films (22.30), the majority of which are good quality.

Also available is the (now famous) Al Jazeera Satellite Channel. This is a home-grown private TV station currently all in Arabic. Referred to as 'the CNN of the Arab world', they have a refreshing independence. Any media company that can make many different countries angry with them simply by trying to portray both sides

4

of a situation must be doing something right. An English service is planned.

The local English-language radio station is QBS, which is on 97.5 and 102.6 FM. It provides a wide variety of programmes for all tastes, including a service in French during the early afternoon. Still not nearly as slick (or glib) as Qatar's more advanced neighbours, the radio service comes in for some criticism, particularly in the winter months when atmospherics make the FM stations of the adjacent countries unobtainable.

Newspapers and Magazines

There are two English-language papers – *The Gulf Times* and *The Peninsula*, both of which are broadsheets and published daily, except Fridays. As well as all the local news, the papers take a great deal of agency material and cover global events, politics, sports, and so on, in reasonable detail. As Gulf papers go, they enjoy considerable freedom from the heavy hand of censorship (which has officially been terminated in Qatar) and can be a lively read, particularly the letters to the Editor. Foreign print media is harder to come by (and expensive) and is sometimes subject to the censor's large black felt tip pen.

People, Practices and Rules

As an Islamic country, Qatar is a conservative place, but it does not impose its values on the visitor. Indeed, in the last few years the atmosphere has changed perceptibly and is more relaxed than in the early 1990s. Alcohol is now available in Western hotels, there is a gentle, easy-going feel to the place and, apart from the minarets which punctuate the skyline and the calls of the muezzin, there is, superficially, little to suggest that you are in a Muslim society where Islam is a powerful force. But you are, and it is important not to lose sight of that fact. The very formation of modern-day Qatar owes its roots to the desire of the Al-Thani tribe to adhere to the code of Islam adopted by the conservative Wahhabi sect.

Islam and Daily Life

Islam means 'active submission to the will of God' and is more than a religion – it is a way of life. A Muslim believes that God's hand is present in every act or occurrence on earth: thus the first Arabic expression you are likely to hear is '*In-Sha Allah*'– 'if God wills'. This is something you will encounter time and time again. It does not imply insouciance or any negativity, it simply means that if God wishes it to come to pass, it will. 'See you tomorrow' will invoke a reply of '*In-Sha Allah*'. The person has every intention of seeing you tomorrow but his or her ability to do so rests with a higher authority.

Jihad (The Holy War)

Jihad is sometimes referred to as the sixth pillar, but is not obligatory and certainly not undertaken by all Muslims. Jihad is probably the most widely misunderstood tenet of Islam. The very word is emotive. These words are misused by both sides. It is well beyond the scope of this guide to advise further save to say that the concept will hardly come into play at any time for the average reader and user.

Etiquette

There are any number of misconceptions about the ground rules when working with Arabs. Travellers' tales about the ease with which one can offend these exotic men in white robes are just that: tales. Gulf Arabs are a tolerant group and know that Westerners – especially first timers – can be nervous and worried about giving offence. More than one new visitor has been so worried that they might inadvertently show the soles of their feet to an Arab that they remain rooted to the spot, unable to show anything to anyone. The best advice is be relaxed. There are some ground rules, but it really is pretty hard to give genuine offence, if you have half a brain. Remember: courtesy, calmness and good manners are much admired here – as they are everywhere.

Tipping

There is no great tipping culture in Qatar – the practices are much in line with the west. Restaurant bills usually come with a service charge included, and, as is the way of the world, a few riyals given to those who make life that little bit easier by lugging stuff about is much appreciated. Some tend to round taxi fares up a bit – others do not. It's a matter of taste.

Conversation Topics

In Britain one is advised that in conversations with people outside your closest circle one should avoid three subjects,

Politics, Religion, and the Royal Family, which possibly explains why the British speak mostly about the weather so much. However, welcome to a major culture shock. After quite a short acquaintance, one will be invited to air views on a whole range of topics that will probably include the three British taboos. It's genuine conversation. If invited, feel free to state your views calmly and quietly and be sure to ask for theirs. Your interlocutor is probably genuinely interested in what you think, or more probably in what your Foreign Minister (for example) really meant when he said whatever he said.

Meeting and Greeting

Always shake hands on meeting and taking leave. Handshakes are important. A firm grasp and honest eye contact are appreciated. You can judge how a meeting has gone by the differing lengths and styles of the 'hello' and 'goodbye' handshake. The 'hello' handshake should be firm and polite enough if it's not you're probably in trouble already. If the 'goodbye' handshake is so insistent that you wonder when the polite moment is to break it, and it also involves the left hand gripping your elbow, then you know that you've scored big time.

Although it may appear the contrary, Arabs are no more tactile than the average Britain. The protocol of the greeting kiss between men is highly formulated and is based on station and personal closeness. Watch carefully at the beginning of the local TV news to get a feel for what is happening. A kiss from a European is not only not expected by an Arab but not welcomed. A vivid picture of how not to do it was portrayed on TV some years ago by Britain's Foreign Minister, seen across the world lunging at a seemingly unprepared and certainly startled Yasser Arafat.

Women

Women will generally find few restrictions in Qatar. They are allowed to drive and there are few problems associated with employment. Visiting businesswomen should encounter no real difficulties – indeed, they may well find themselves received with more courtesy and interest than in the West.

European women do not shake hands, and certainly do not offer a cheek to be kissed. If you are introduced to a local lady, men should not attempt to shake hands unless a hand is offered.

4

Five Pillars of Islam

Since its birth in 622, the religion of Islam has been based on five branches, called the Five Pillars. The first of these is the most important, and the fundamental tenet of being a Muslim. The other four are generally observed by Muslims, although non-observance of them does not constitute a departure from Islam.

Islam being an essential part of life in Qatar, it is important for any traveller visiting the country to have some idea of its basics.

The Five Pillars are:

1. The *Shahadah* (Faith): The most important pillar is the practice and observance of a chant-like declaration pronouncing that there is no god other than God (*Allah*), and that His messenger is Muhammad (Peace be upon Him - pbuh), as explained earlier. The message of the chant is that nothing in life (including material things like wealth or power) should take precedence over God.

2. *Salah* (Prayers): These are canonical prayers performed daily. They contain verses from the Qur'an, and are spoken in Arabic. They are led by a learned person who knows the Qur'an, and are seen as a direct link between the worshipper and God.

3. *Zakah* (Generosity): *Zakah* translates into 'purification' and 'growth'. It is based on the premise that all things belong to God, and that part of one's earnings must thus be distributed to the poor. *Zakah* is usually two and a half per cent of a Muslim's income, but may be calculated individually.

4. *Sawm* (Fasting): For the month of Ramadan, Muslims observe a fast, which constitutes abstinence from food, drink and sexual relations between sunrise and sundown. The purpose of this fast is to allow for spiritual growth, as well as to experience empathy with those who hunger.

Hajj (Pilgrimage to Mecca): This is an annual pilgrimage to Makkah (Mecca), to be undertaken only by those physically and financially able to do so at least once during a lifetime. Pilgrims wear simple cloth garments, so as to stand equally before God, without class or wealth distinction.

4

Hospitable Beverages

First things first: be prepared for the intake of larger volumes of liquid than you are accustomed to. Use the bathroom before you leave your hotel in order to be ready to accept coffee or tea or whatever else whenever offered. It is bad manners to refuse. Even if you are in your 10th meeting of the day and your bladder is bursting, have a small cup of something. Hospitality is at the very heart of society in this part of the world. You may be looking forward to an ice-cold beer back in your five-star hotel, but in the DNA of your host, you have just ridden miles across the desert under a blazing sun on the back of a grumpy camel. He will expect you to have a drink and be surprised and offended if you do not. In Qatar, you may be offered any number of alternatives to the endless tea, including yogurt drinks and herbal infusions. Take an interest, ask what they are and try them out. One good tip to remember is not to ask for sugar unless you have a very sweet tooth. If you are asked 'with sugar?' respond: 'a little'; that way you'll only get a heaped teaspoon instead of a desert spoonful.

4

Body Language

It is highly offensive to show the bottom of the foot to an Arab (they are considered – and indeed they sometimes are – unclean). Just bear it in mind and try to relax – which is preferred by your hosts. Only the right hand should be used for anything remotely interesting – certainly for accepting or giving food and business cards – even making gestures during conversation. The left hand is used for more personal purposes.

While on the subject of business cards, work out how many you'll need for the trip, double it, and then double it again. Have your details in English on one side and Arabic on the other. Beware of beckoning with the forefinger - it has unfortunate connotations. In fact, avoid beckoning altogether. And that old travellers' tale of not admiring something, as the owner will be obliged to offer it as a gift, has some truth.

Dress Sense

Qatar is, as we have noted, a conservative, Islamic country and this is reflected in its dress codes – both for men and women. No-one is expected to be covered at all times from head to toe, but all should display modesty and decency in their style of dress. This is largely a question of common sense, though for some reason some visitors seem to live in blissful ignorance of their surroundings. For men, avoid shorts and vests except in the appropriate sporting arenas. Trousers, slacks, jeans, etc. are fine. Real shirts, please,except on the beach or by the pool. As for women, wear below-the-knee skirts and dresses, and avoid showing your shoulders.

Alcohol

Muslims are forbidden to drink alcohol and it is an offence to buy alcohol for a Muslim. Non-Muslims can obtain alcohol in the major Western hotels; non-Muslim residents may obtain a liquor licence, which allows a certain amount of alcohol to be purchased from a bonded supplier. Trade in alcohol is strictly prohibited and the offence carries a prison sentence and deportation. When dining with or entertaining local nationals and other Muslims, assume that drinking in their presence will not be acceptable.

All (non-medicinal, so-called recreational) drugs are prohibited and their use and/or sale carries stern punishment. Do not bring these into the country nor offer them to your Qatari guests when you meet them in Europe.

4

What's in a Name?

And those names! Which bit do you use? This is important, as names have a significance in the Arab world beyond that of the West. Study them and use them to understand the family relationships, as do the locals. Some names sound and look very similar, but Mohammed is different to Mahmoud. When writing to an Arab, use the transliteration they use (and note that Mohammed is sometimes contracted to 'Mohd').

Gulf Arabs' names are usually broken down as follows: personal name followed by the father's name, then the grandfather's name. An alternative is the personal name, followed by the father's name, and then the tribal name. For example, Abdullah bin Ahmed bin Salman or Abdullah bin Ahmed al-Darwish. 'Bin' means 'son of'. 'Abu' means 'father of', so Adbullah bin Ahmed's father Ahmed might well be known to his friends as Abu Abdullah. While it may seem complicated, strive to understand since names and relationships are important.

If you meet a member of the Al-Thani family, the correct title is 'Sheikh', with the personal name, and for ladies, 'Sheikha', followed by her personal name. If he is a senior member, 'Your Excellency' or 'Your Highness', is a safe form of address.

The Calendar

In common with most of the rest of the Arab world, Qatar acknowledges the Gregorian (Western) calendar and uses this for business and everyday life. However, the daily round for Muslims and the year is driven by the Islamic or *hejira* calendar. This dates from the flight of the Prophet Mohammed to Medina, and is based on the lunar cycle. There are 354 days in the *hejira* year, with no adjusting leap year, so everything moves against the fixed dates of the Gregorian calendar by 11 days each cycle. The annual Islamic event of *Hajj*, the pilgrimage to Makkah, moves forward each year by eleven days, as do the other notable Islamic events of *Eid al Adha* (at the end of *Hajj*), Ramadan, and *Eid al Fitr* (at the end of Ramadan).

Ramadan

The key feature of the Islamic calendar is the Holy Month of Ramadan. Muslims observing Ramadan will not eat, drink or smoke during daylight hours. They will eat just before sunrise and not break their fast again until the sun sets. At that time, the celebratory breaking the fast meal of *iftar* takes place. Most hotels and restaurants have special *iftar* menus. The chances are that if you are in town during Ramadan you will be invited to join your hosts for the meal. Accept.

For those trying to conduct business, Ramadan can be a frustrating time, as the dislocation felt by those observing the fast becomes evident in working life. Although it is not impossible to do business during Ramadan, it is, on the whole, best avoided, if at all possible.

If you are in Qatar during Ramadan, you must avoid eating, drinking and smoking in public during daylight hours. If your host offers refreshment at meetings, it is polite gently to decline. This acknowledgement of an important religious time will be noted and appreciated. You will almost certainly find that restrictions apply on the sale of alcohol during Ramadan, although you will

4

probably be able to obtain a midday meal in your room or a secluded part of the hotel.

Public Holidays

Eid simply means holiday. There are two each year, which are based on the Islamic calendar and depend on local lunar sightings. Holidays are thus uncertain as to precise date of commencement. These holidays are officially four days in duration, but the Government offices and the banks normally take considerably longer.

Below is a guide to the movable public holidays over the next few years:

	2002	2003	2004
Islamic New Year	15 Mar	5 Mar	22 Feb
Ramadan starts	6 Nov	27 Oct	15 Oct
Eid Al Fitr	6 Dec	26 Nov	14 Nov
Eid Al Adha	23 Feb	12 Feb	2 Feb

(Neither the Islamic New Year, nor any birthdays, including that of the prophet Muhammad, is celebrated as a holiday in Qatar.)

The Working Week

For the shops, retail outlets and *suqs* the working week is essentially six-and-a-half days with only Friday mornings being closed. Shops tend to be open from 0900 to 1200 and 1600 to anywhere from 2000 to midnight! Supermarkets and malls stay open throughout the day.

Private businesses mostly work a five-and-half-day week with Thursday afternoon and Friday being the days off. Working weeks are usually 0800 to 1300 and 1600 to 1900. However, with the move led by the oil and gas industry and followed by the banks, there is pressure on private companies and contractors to move to a Friday/Saturday weekend. This would require a major shift in attitude and the likelihood of it happening quickly is remote.

The oil and gas sector, following the lead of the national oil company, Qatar Petroleum, now work a five-day week with Friday and Saturday being the weekend. Timings are 0700 to 1500.

4

The banks are formally open from 0730 to 1300 Sunday to Thursday, with local branch differences to accommodate customer's needs.

Prayers

Muslims pray five times a day at: sunrise, mid-morning, mid-afternoon, sunset and an hour after sunset. These prayer times vary according to the lunar cycle and therefore length of the day. Whilst business does not come to a grinding stop and shops close as in Saudi Arabia, it is quite possible the individual you wish to speak to, or even are speaking to, will wish to interrupt the (your) flow for prayers. This may be short or involve a visit to the local mosque. It is wise to be aware of the times of prayer each day (not difficult since they are printed in the daily papers) and try to plan your time around them. If you are conducting a seminar or lengthy group meeting, always adjust the pauses for coffee, etc., to coincide with prayer times.

Weather

4

The climate in Qatar is very pleasant from October to April, with temperatures in the teens and upper 20s centigrade. The summer months, however, become furnace-like, with 40° to 50°c shade temperature the norm during the day and not much cooler at night. Qatar does not experience the oppressive, continual, high humidity found in other Gulf countries, and for most of the time the air is reasonably dry. There are also sandstorms in midsummer, and it is not unknown for there to be sudden rain and electrical storms, with thunder, lightning and localised torrential downpours.

There is a real rainy season when Qatar can expect to catch the tail end of the Asian Monsoons. These two periods are November/December and February/March. The second period tends to be more predictable but either period may not occur at all. The rain may be fleeting and localised or even heavy and widespread for days.

It is still the case that business more or less shuts down for the summer between mid-July and mid-September, as most locals retreat to cooler climes though these days more and more companies maintain a year-round working presence. Summer 2002 has seen an effort on the part of the Government to encourage people to spend less

time away with its 'Summer Surprises' shopping and
entertainment packages.

Food and Medical Care

Eating and drinking

Chapter Eight gives details of eating out, but the great
thing is that these days food and beverage options in
Qatar are becoming increasingly varied. The choices
range from top-of-the-range dining in the five-star hotels
to much more modest fare in the plethora of restaurants
all over the city serving Arabic, Pakistani, Indian, Thai,
Chinese and fast-food meals. Many of them are pretty
basic in style and décor, and the quality of food can be
variable. But standards of hygiene are high and it is
unlikely that you will suffer should you experiment a
little.

While Western (and Eastern) visitors have a wide choice
of restaurants offering fare from home, it would be a pity
not to try Arabic food and the local seafood while in
Qatar. The local cuisine – with heavy Lebanese
influences – is simple by nature: salads, pickled
vegetables, grilled meat, bread, fish and fruit are the
staples – but the very simplicity of the food allows the
true taste to emerge. You should aim to try *mezze* at
least once. This is a variety of small dishes – olives,
salads, dips made from chickpeas and other groundnuts,
plus the most wonderful bread. Main courses include
kebabs of lamb, chicken or seafood, marinated, skewered
and grilled, and served with rice.

Try to have some *ghuzi* (lamb roasted whole),
matchbous (spiced lamb with rice) and some *hammour*,
(the local white fish, which is superb). Gulf seafood,
crustaceans, is highly recommended. If you have any
room for dessert, you must try *Umm Ali* a fantastic
bread pudding which has to be tasted to be believed.
Whether Ali's mother (the translation) really dreamed up
the recipe is the subject of fierce historical debate, but
whoever did invent *Umm Ali* deserves a place in the
culinary hall of fame.

Street food is delicious and usually safe to eat. Try a
chicken or lamb *shawarma* – slow-grilled meat, sliced
and folded into a piece of unleavened bread with a
dollop of salad and dressing.

4

Medical care

Qatar is pretty well equipped when it comes to healthcare. The main establishment is the Hamad Hospital, which is a busy and bustling place. It deals with all manner of ailments but mostly serves the victims of traffic accidents (see above!). Accident and emergency facilities are good and attention is quick. If the worst happens and you have to summon help quickly, dial 999 and give a coherent account of what has happened and what you need. The emergency services are fast and efficient and speak English. The standard of hospital care is also good, with mostly Indian doctors (increasingly augmented by newly-qualified Qatari nationals) and Filipina nurses. There is any number of doctors and dentists practising in downtown Doha. Surprisingly the English actress Susan George has a thriving practice in the *suq* zone – or perhaps it's her namesake.

For the usual traveller's aches and pains, your hotel will be able to arrange access to a doctor.

The handicapped traveller

Qatar is becoming increasingly sensitive to the needs of the handicapped traveller and more and more facilities are being introduced in key buildings. It has to be said that they have not caught up with the best standards of Europe or North America, but things are improving. If you are less than mobile and are planning a business trip, it would be as well to do as much advance planning as possible. The recently opened Intercontinental Hotel is proud of its ability to cater for the disadvantaged traveller and many of the older hotels, like the Ramada, are taking particular care in this area when it comes to refurbishing.

New District of Doha

Diplomatic Area

Al Bidr Road

Rayyan Road

Bread Street

Al-Sadd
Roundabout

Musheireb Street

A RING ROAD

B RING ROAD

Road

5

getting down to business

getting down to business

This chapter provides elementary
guidance on the basic etiquette of
business, and also contains details
of useful local organisations who
can assist with the more
complicated requirements of
business transactions.

GETTING DOWN TO BUSINESS

Business Etiquette

In Chapter Four we looked at the general social mores and customs in Qatar. Now it is time to consider them in a business context. Before we start, keep in mind that in Qatar progress of almost any kind, and decision-making in particular, proceed at a snail's pace. The best advice is to be patient, but be prepared. Stay in touch, with your target in mind, and continue to do your homework, because when the decision comes be expected to respond instantly.

The first contact

The essence of any business relationship in Qatar, the Gulf or indeed the Arab world, is personal contact. This applies most assuredly to any contact you have with nationals but also applies, in general, to contact with middlemen, whether from the UK, the sub-continent or anywhere else. You cannot service this market by remote control. Trust and personal chemistry are vital to the successful pursuit of business here.

The first meeting between you and your prospective customer/buyer/agent is hugely important. The first few minutes will dictate how well – or badly – the relationship develops, though, it may take some time actually to get to that first meeting, as the keeping of business engagements in the Gulf can be a hit-and-miss affair. Having made your initial appointment, gently check from time to time (by phone) that it is still on course. And having established a definite time and place, get there in good time and be prepared to wait.

Knowing and recognising your target

Meetings in the Gulf can be exquisitely confusing, and Qatar is no exception. The first few people you meet may have nothing to do with the meeting at all. But they will convey you ever nearer to the inner sanctum where the person you are really meeting will be. Pay attention at this point, because he is unlikely to be alone. Try to fix in your mind the name of the person you are meant to be talking to, and during the ceremonial handing over of business cards identify him. This may sound bizarre, but if you are not used to meeting men in white robes in a flurry of handshakes, it is easy to go wrong. It is not unusual to spend many minutes agreeably chatting to someone who has nothing to do with the business at

5

hand, but is a cousin who has dropped in for a chat and coffee.

You would be forgiven for thinking all Gulf Arabs look alike, when you meet several Arabs briefly (perhaps at a social function shortly after you arrive) and then have to remember who is who the following day, when they all had similar names (which you didn't quite grasp), build and dress. A simple visual mnemonic like a 'fat bloke with gold pen in pocket' or 'thin chap, interesting cufflinks on his *dishdasha*' is sometimes useful. Make sure you swap a card, and memorize the face, starting at the nose and working your way out to see the whole visage. The rest doesn't matter. The dress won't help and next time he may be sitting down or standing up, or even in Western clothing with a bare head, in which case even the most seasoned professional can get it wrong! Studying the face also helps you with making eye contact, essential on the first contact as noted earlier.

It is good to be able to say a few words of greeting in Arabic as you enter and shake hands. Starting with a few simple greetings like *assalam alaikum* or *wa alaikum assalam* in response if he says it first, and the enquiry *kayf halek* to ask how he is, will break the ice and show the right spirit. It will then allow you to say 'I'm ashamed to say that's all the Arabic I speak', in a (hopefully) disarming way.

Business cards

The exchange of business cards must take place. As mentioned in Chapter Four, you can never have too many cards in the Gulf. They will disappear at an alarming rate. It creates a good impression if you have Arabic on one side. Just make sure that you have had the Arabic done professionally by someone reliable. One person was on his second box of cards before it was pointed out that the Arabic, while correct, had another person's name on it! He was new to the company and had left it to 'administration' to arrange, using a colleague's card. He had changed his name in English and received a 'yes, of course' to the question: 'can you do the Arabic?' (It was a French company. Obviously more than he bargained for had been lost in the translation.)

When accepting someone's card, do not just shove it in your pocket. Read it, and make a show of so doing, perhaps by asking a question about it or the contents. Keep it in your hand or put it on the table in front of you and don't forget to take it with you on departure. That person's card says a lot about them and they appreciate your paying it some attention.

Opening moves

Pleasantries follow and they can be as inane as you like. Tell them how hot you find it – as the damp patches work their way through your shirt this might not be strictly necessary. Don't ask about wife and family – you don't know them well enough. Keep it general. If Qatar won (or lost) at soccer recently, that would be a good one to throw in. Any soccer reference is usually safe ground (a bit like the English and the weather) – most nationals have a favourite English team, and, amazingly, it is not always Manchester United. A good idea is to have a quick look at the local news in that morning's newspaper and have one or two stories to bring up or observations to make. It shows that you are interested in Qatar.

5

Then a man will appear from nowhere and you will be asked what you would like to drink. Depending on where you are, the drinks on offer might include Western tea/coffee ('Nescafe'), Turkish coffee, Arabic tea ('shay'), water, Coke, orange, etc. Then (if not before) another man will offer you Arabic coffee ("kahwah") which is a small tot of an exotic infusion involving coffee beans and cardomom, etc. which is a pleasant, if perhaps acquired, taste. It is considered obligatory to have one cup and even two if you like it. Signify that you have had your fill by shaking the little cup when the coffee man comes by. This sounds faintly embarrassing but is easily mastered. Say shukran (thank you) to the tea-boy. It shows respect and is often noted by the host.

The arrival of the drinks is usually the signal to get down to business. The scope of the conversation will, of course, vary from case to case, but there are some generalities that it might be as well to observe:

● Time is usually on their side. If you are in 'sell' mode, it is important to bear this in mind. They know you have a plane to catch and will position themselves accordingly. You can disarm them by having a flexible itinerary.

- They want to deal with decision-makers and are not impressed by the 'I'll have to clear that with head office' line. Know your authority.
- They respect straight but gentle talking. The worst thing you can do is lose your temper or appear immoderate in any way. They admire calmness and a wry sense of humour, but don't tell jokes.
- Don't be thrown or annoyed if your host answers the phone or even makes a call in the middle of the meeting. And other people in the room may be doing the same thing. Underlings will come in to obtain signatures. There will be gentle mayhem. Best to let it wash over you in a Zen-like way.
- Speak simply and clearly but not in a patronising way. Do not use slang or colloquial terms. Speak evenly and don't get excited or agitated. Loss of composure in any way is seen as somewhat vulgar.
- If you are making a presentation, keep it clear, succinct and short. Punchiness without razzamatazz is what you should be seeking to achieve. Think carefully about the use of illustrations – girls, alcohol and pork (separately or together) should be avoided.
- Use Arabic in written material. Even if your translation budget does not stretch to having extensive product literature in Arabic, at least have a summary sheet done. It may not be strictly necessary but it is an excellent sign of serious intent and consideration. Whatever you choose to translate, use a first-class translator. You will see many examples of imaginative English phrases and spelling, from which you'll get a chuckle. Given any one word for translation and any two locals from different parts and you will get several versions and endless arguments about what is correct. Written material should be simple and well illustrated. Glossy and colourful is good.
- Beware of throwaway remarks, especially if they could be construed as offers. These can be interpreted as binding and could fatally damage trust if they have to be withdrawn. Remember the importance of the spoken word, which was mentioned earlier.
- Be prepared to bargain, but avoid starting with what will look like a rip-off price if you come down dramatically. But know the worth of your product and make it clear.
- You will rarely hear the word 'no'. But its absence does not mean 'yes'. Although this sounds laborious and time-

consuming (and it can be), remember that once a deal is struck it is almost always honoured. Speaking of which, remember that business matters are considered very private and a matter only for the parties involved. If your business partner discovers that you have been blathering about the deal all over town, you will be dead in the water (figuratively speaking of course this isn't Sicily).

● Keep any written agreements simple and clear. Local law will prevail if – and try to avoid this at all costs – matters go to court.

Representation

Do not believe you can do without representation in whatever form. Qatar is a village where everyone knows everyone elses business (or think they do). Business works on the personal level and one of the key ingredients is trust. Trust is developed by years of being present, getting a solid reputation for getting it right, and showing you are serious and reliable. You may have all those qualities in your other markets but in Qatar you are an unknown quantity until you prove yourself. You won't have the time to do that, nor the time to develop all the personal contacts, information sources and door-openers needed to make the market work. You can short cut the process with the right sort of representation.

'E Commerce?', 'My business does not need to be in the Country', 'I can do it all via the Internet'. Don't delude yourself. Though switched on with the Internet, phones and e-mail and there are one or two local companies who have dabbled for local supply of local goods and services, even that hasn't taken off. You may be able to process the orders via the Internet, but it is unlikely that the business will come without someone locally pressing the flesh and drinking the tea.

There are many ways you can approach representation. These vary from working in an informal (that is unregistered) way with an individual or company, through to formal representation with an agreement registered with the Chamber of Commerce, or to a local company formed by a formal joint venture. In deciding what is appropriate, and therefore what type of organisation you want to associate with, the best advice is to decide what you want to achieve now, in 12 months and in 5 years.

5

If you are essentially a business looking to carry out contracting or manufacturing, you have very little option but to accept that you need to be present. There are softer options to allow you to put your toes in the water, the most common of which is to agree to a 'sponsorship' arrangement with a local company. Such arrangements fall short of proper joint ventures, with the formation of a company jointly held between your company and a local partner – more of which in Chapter Seven. Such arrangements should never be seen as an end in themselves, but as a stepping stone towards the future.

A word of caution on sponsorship arrangements: the usual method is to register your business as a branch of an existing company, which allows your business to open a bank account, claim a local Commercial Registration (CR) Number, bid on local contracts as a local company, and trade. However, be sure that the local business and the name chosen will be 100 per cent the property of your local partner, just in case something goes wrong.

5

Selling a product is a lot simpler. By far the most common way of marketing goods is through the use of an agent or distributor. As is the case throughout the Gulf, the choice of agent is crucial, not simply from the point of view of business success but because getting rid of an agent is not easy. Throughout the Gulf laws regarding commercial agencies have been reviewed and have been relaxed, making the regulations less biased in favour of the agent. Qatar is no different and a new law was enacted in June 2002.

Proper old Gulf hands (not someone with a couple of years' experience in overseas markets as a part of their corporate work experience profile for Human Resources) sometimes say ruefully that getting an agent is like getting married – relatively simple to do, complicated to undo. It's a relationship that is meant to be for life, and the good ones are. Although the new law does make it clearer and simpler, termination can be difficult and expensive.

There will be no shortage of people in Qatar who want to be your agent. Perhaps they really can do a great job for you. Perhaps they have fantastic connections. Perhaps they simply want to represent your product to prevent competition for the rival product for which they are also the agent. The Trade Partners UK team in the

Commercial Department of the British Embassy can help you. They know all the players in town and will be happy to give an opinion on people you are thinking of appointing.

Evaluating an agent

What do you look for in an agent? Size and strength of operation. Length of time they have been trading. Portfolio of business and other agencies. Will they be able to get you new business? How do they intend to market your product? Do they have good links with government? Can they keep you up to date with changes in regulations? Beware of claims from an agent who says he can represent you right across the Gulf or even right across the spectrum of business in Qatar. He cannot. All have their circles of friends and influence which cannot be sidestepped.

Legal issues

Before embarking on acquiring an agent, it is best to get up-to-date information on agency law. Any good law firm with Gulf representation will be able to help and, having found a partner to work with and done your homework, check it all out with one of them. As with any form of business contract in the Gulf (or anywhere else) get the best advice you can before committing yourself. There are a number of first-class legal firms who can offer this type of service and some are suggested at the end of this chapter.

Keep the following information, tips and points in mind:

● The law that governs the activities of agents and all that goes with them is Commercial Agency Law No 8 of 2002, which, on 9 June 2002, replaced previous Law No 4 of 1986.
● Do not sign up with the first prospective agent you meet, no matter how persuasive.
● Seek proper legal advice.
● Liaise with any help you can find on the ground – e.g. the TPUK team at the British Embassy if you are British.
● Negotiate performance measures and do not be shy about doing so.
● Do not use the word 'exclusive' unless it is essential, and after you have taken legal advice.
● Agree to an initial trial period.

5

- Find out who else your prospective agent represents.
- Avoid litigation, it is lengthy, costly and you will almost certainly lose one way or another.

Trade and Trading Conditions in Qatar

Qatar is a fairly open country especially when it comes to business. However, there are rules and regulations governing overseas trade. The Market Desk at Trade Partners UK (as noted, ❑ Tel: +44 207 215 5444), has up-to-the-minute information on the current regime, but what follows is a general guide to the arrangements.

Free-Trade Zones and arrangements

Qatar has no free trade zones for re-export or for manufacture. On the other hand, along with Saudi Arabia, Kuwait, Bahrain, UAE and Oman, Qatar is a member of the Gulf Cooperation Council (GCC). Although not a fully-fledged customs union, membership of the GCC allows it to participate in a free-trade agreement, providing duty-free access to goods produced in the other GCC countries. In addition, Qatar is a member of The Arab League, which has recently agreed to negotiate an Arab Free-Trade Zone, but the effect and benefits of that arrangement are still some way off.

Import Controls

For the rest of the world, exporting to Qatar is more complex as this is where the various stringent laws come into play. These rules are not necessarily those of Qatar. Notably, in these troubled times, restrictions on hi-tech equipment may be controlled from the point of export. Local information, at both ends, should be taken on board at the earliest opportunity.

Banned products

It is important to be aware of the restrictions applying to the import of certain goods into Qatar. Religious or politically sensitive goods may not be imported into the country at all, and you can be sure that any questionable goods will certainly be thoroughly scrutinised by Qatari censors.

In keeping with Islamic law, pork and pork derivatives may not be imported. Beef and poultry must be accompanied by all the correct health certificates, in addition to a *Halal* slaughter certificate, issued from the country of origin to confirm that the animal has been slaughtered according to Islamic rites. Alcohol is only imported and distributed by the Qatar Distribution Company, who run the duty-free shopping areas at the airport and 'the booze shop' as it is colloquially known. Qatar Distribution Company is a part of Qatar Airways.

Documentation

Goods imported by air, land and sea must all be accompanied by specific documentation in the form of letters of credit and bills of lading. Your shipping company or agent will be able to assist you. To obtain up-to-date information on this, contact Trade Partners UK.

Customs Duties

Qatar has adopted a policy of exemption from customs duty on items related to the construction of infrastructure, foods and personal properties. It imposes a duty of 4 per cent on other items, whereas the duties on items competing with locally-produced items reach as high as 30 per cent for urea and 20 per cent for iron and steel as a way of protecting national industry. The customs duty on tobacco is 100 per cent and on musical instruments 15 per cent.

Labelling

Labelling is another specific area that requires attention. Labels (particularly on food) must comply with set rules covering the provision of detailed product information on all labels, and must be in Arabic. All food products must have a production and expiry date and outlets can be severely penalised for offering foodstuffs for sale beyond the date stamped on the container. This stricture leads to regular bargain sales close to a product's expiry date. It also leads to the rather anomalous labelling recently seen on a package labelled 'Genuine Rock Salt mined from deposits laid down 200 million years ago' and overprinted 'Expiry Date 04 August 2002'.

Trademarks

Trade and service marks are protected under the provisions of the Qatar Trademarks Law Number 3 of 1978 and its Implementing Regulations Number 30 of 1980. This covers the protection of marks of non-Qatari nationals. It does not require evidence of prior use in Qatar or elsewhere.

The trademark is registered with the Trademark Office of the Commercial Affairs Department at the Ministry of Economy and Commerce. The process of registration takes somewhere in the region of two to three years from the date of submission of an application in the proper form to the Trademarks registry.

Copyright

Intellectual property rights are protected under the Qatar Copyright Law Number 25 of 1995. This covers original works of literature, art and science, and protects both Qataris and non-Qataris who are from countries with which Qatar has reciprocal arrangements. The major publicly seen area is in pirated music videos and software and the Copyright Office make regular raids on outlets and cottage businesses churning out these products. However, they are active across the board, when policing of claims made of copyright infringement is called for.

Patents

Patent law is a part of the GCC Patent Regulation and Implementing by e-laws, which were established in 1992 and ratified in Qatar by Emiri Decree Number 46 of 1996. While the Ministry of Economy and Commerce does accept patent applications they are actually sent to Riyadh in Saudi Arabia for review.

Passing Off and Unfair Competition

This is covered via the Qatar Civil and Commercial Law Number 16 of 1971. Suffice it to say there is a structure on which the businessman can hang his argument. The best advice is: don't go down that road in a legal sense. Better to use the weight of your friends and 'representative' to guide you and the miscreant to a sensible solution.

How to promote your wares

Advertising

Neither advertising nor publishing in Qatar can be considered major industries, although both have somewhere to go and there are signs that this is happening. Both are hamstrung by the size of the markets and the perception by local advertisers of what advertising is and does and therefore their attitude towards cost/benefit. Most advertising is still carried out in the daily newspapers and on billboards. Both Radio and TV have made attempts to promote themselves as valid alternatives but seemingly with little success. There are a growing number of subject specific periodicals produced locally or produced in the neighbouring countries and targeting the Qatari market. Also on the plus side, while promotional opportunities and vehicles do improve sales, rates for advertising in all media still tend to be extremely attractive in comparison to the rates found elsewhere in the Gulf. See Chapter Two for some specific contact addresses for advertising.

Exhibitions and Seminars

Exhibition trade shows have not yet made a strong showing in Qatar, at least not as far as international events are concerned. The Doha Oil and Gas Show in the spring is perhaps the most significant. But Qatar seems determined to get its slice of the action and so exhibitions may yet become a valuable way of doing business in the market. But, for the moment, most companies see the world-class shows and facilities in Dubai as the best shop window for Qatar and the rest of the Gulf.

From time to time there are catalogue exhibitions in the Gulf run by the Bristol-based company Supercatex, in association with Trade Partners UK:

❑ Tel: +44 117 909 9990
Website: [www.supercatex.com]

For around £300, they will display your product literature in a suitable venue (usually the local Chamber of Commerce or a major hotel) and hand a copy to *bona fide* business visitors, in return for a business card. They then tell you who has expressed an interest in your product, which in turn provides you with a number of hot leads. Catalogue shows tend to last for three or four days and in Qatar catalogue exhibitions have recently formed part of wider British events, which has helped publicity. The Supercatex concept is an ideal way to test the market and it is only available to companies not already represented in the market – thus it is a happy hunting-ground for agents on the lookout for attractive new products.

A common and most effective way to present and promote is by seminar. Many companies use this method to reach a specific part of their market target directly. It is a most useful way to start the ball rolling. Once again, it

5

is necessary to do your homework and ensure that you not only know the companies you want to present to, but individuals in those companies as well. This is an area where the local representative should really excel (if he doesn't perhaps, you should reconsider your options). Once you have the 'hit-list', an arrangement is made with any of the hotels for a suitably sized room, along with the entire projection paraphernalia and audio-visuals required. All the hotels offer the service to varying degrees of quality and cost. The venue and facilities usually come free, or very cheaply, as long as you book several coffee/tea breaks and a meal for the attendees. Unless you have a very unusual product which people are climbing over each other to discover, the hospitality (meal) is the essential key to ensuring that delegates come and stay. A clear indication of the interest and immediate success of the seminar is the number and importance of people who stay beyond the meal.

Help and Information Sources

5

You are in Qatar. This is a business-friendly and welcoming place. Being the well-organised professional that you are, you will have followed all the advice given in Chapter Two and you will be armed with several starting points for your business mission. But you still need friends when you hit the streets and start to make contacts.

British Embassy Commercial Section

Business people or people representing a company have the commercial team at their Embassy as best friends. If you have done your homework, you may have had some contact with the Embassy personnel before your visit but it is still sensible to let them know you are in town and arrange to call in. One complaint they often make is that the call comes when the visitor has already been in town for a while or even about to leave. If you are going to involve the Embassy, get them into your schedule early and get their briefing before you visit potential customers and partners. You pay for them, you might as well use them. In the case of the British Embassy, their alert team is located away from the main Embassy compound near the airport in the Toyota Towers, a local landmark.

❑ Tel: +974 435 3543
E-mail: [bembcomm@qatar.net.qa]

British Council

The British Council is another local source of help. The Council exists to further British influence in a cultural sense and much of their resources are devoted to the teaching of English and the promotion of Britain as a centre of educational excellence. The Council used to have a sandals-and-spectacles reputation, but these days it is very much a business and can offer an excellent way into the schools, universities and training fields. Located conveniently on the quiet end of Al Sadd Street, a fast developing major retail street.

❑ Tel: +974 442 6193/4; fax: +974 442 3315
E-mail: [info@qa.britishcouncil.org]

Chamber of Commerce

Established in 1990, Qatar's Chamber of Commerce aims to promote and aid commercial, industrial and agricultural sectors of Qatar. It provides services to traders, including vital information on trade practices and rules, and participates in trade conferences. It is equipped with helpful Qatari nationals who will assist you in trade queries.

The Chamber of Commerce
Airport Road
PO Box 402, Doha
❑ Tel: +974 4621131; fax: +974 4622538
E-mail: [qcci@qatar.net.qa]

The Qatar British Business Forum
Always ready with advice and support. Contact with the Embassy will often result in a reference to the QBBF or one of its members. The QBBF have no fixed office for visitors, but you can communicate directly with the secretary who will assist and guide you.

❑ Tel: 432 6211; fax: 442 5682
E-mail: [qbbf@qatar.net.qa]

Some suggsted starting points

The following are not by any means lists, nor do they necessarily indicate any better level of performance over their competitors, beyond being prominent and professional (and members of the QBBF). They are but a starting point. Further useful numbers can be found in Appendix One.

5

Legal Practices

Law offices of Gebran Majdalany
PO Box 4004, Doha
❑ Tel: 442 8899; fax: 441 7817
E-mail: [tariq@qatar.net.qa].

Law offices of Dr. Najeeb bin Mohammed Al-Nauimi
In association with Richards Butler
PO Box 9952, Doha
❑ Tel: 431 1124; fax: 431 0314
E-mail: [nnrblaw@qatar.net.qa]

Audit and Accounting

Ernst and Young
PO Box 164, Doha
❑ Tel: 441 4599; fax: 441 44649
E-mail: [eydoha@qatar.net.qa]

Shipping Companies

Gulf Agency Qatar
PO Box 6534, Doha
❑ Tel: 431 5222; fax: 431 4222
E-mail: [qatar.ops@gulfagencycompnay.com]

Document Courier Companies

United Parcel Services (UPS)
PO Box 22062, Doha
❑ Tel: 432 2444; fax: 443 3057
E-mail: [upsqat@qatar.net.qa]

DHL Qatar (International) Ltd
PO Box 9520, Doha
❑ Tel: 462 1202; fax: 462 2020
E-mail: [dohtrc@dxb-co.ae.dhl.com]

5

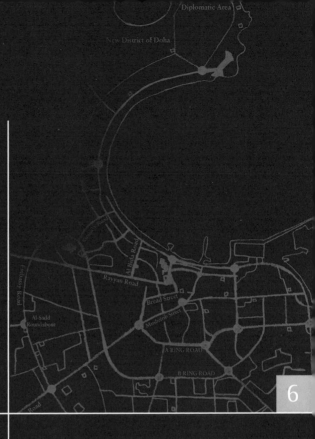

Major industries

6

Major industries

An overview of each of the major
industries of the nation and
where they stand today.

Export and import activity is at the heart of Qatar's economy. As with many of the Gulf's oil and gas producers, Qatar's economy is essentially a simple trade of oil and gas in return for everything else. Local manufacture is limited. Tourism currently accounts for only one-half of one per cent of the Gross National Product. Income from the sale of hydrocarbon products finances all public spending and is the fuel for Qatar's growing investment portfolio.

Qatar is a member of the following international organisations:
The United Nations (UN)
The Organisation of Petroleum Producing Countries (OPEC)
The Organisation of the Arab Petroleum Exporting Countries (OAPEC)
The Arab League
The International Monetary Fund (IMF)
The World Bank
The World Trade Organisation (WTO)
The World Intellectual Property Organisation (WIPO)

Qatar has 35 diplomatic Embassies abroad and 35 Diplomatic Representatives in Qatar.

Qatar's mature and responsible approach to foreign affairs has led to the establishment of excellent relations with a great number of nations and this in turn has underpinned trading activity. Qatar's major export market for crude oil is Japan, while China and India offer excellent markets for fertiliser and petrochemical products. Japan and Korea are the main markets for its burgeoning LNG (liquefied natural gas) trade. Qatar's traditional sources of imports are the US, UK and Japan. Main imports are: capital equipment associated with oil and gas development, vehicles, foodstuffs, luxury items, electronic equipment, manufactured goods plus construction and contract furnishing requirements. Goods deemed necessary to the national interest can be imported tariff-free, but in general a 4 per cent import tax applies. Goods that compete against local manufacture (steel, cement, and urea for example) attract a 20 per cent tariff, while tobacco goods are taxed at 100 per cent.

Oil and Gas

Successful exploitation of Qatar's oil and gas deposits is at the very heart of the nation's economic strength.

6

Although efforts are under way to introduce economic and commercial diversification, hydrocarbons will, for the foreseeable future, dominate the Qatari economy.

Oil

Oil started the creation of modern Qatar. Although exploration for oil started in 1923, the first discoveries were not made until 1939 in what became known as the Dukhan field. This field remains the backbone of Qatar's oil production but has since been joined by at least six offshore oil fields – the latest field to come on stream was the al-Karkara offshore field in 1998. Although production started almost immediately after discovery, the Second World War meant Qatar had to wait another 10 years before the first exports of oil took place. The timely discovery and exploitation of oil occurred just as the pearl fishing industry was being extinguished by the introduction of cultivated pearls from Japan.

Around 50 per cent of Qatar's crude output still comes from this source which is operated solely by Qatar Petroleum – until January 2001 known as QGPC – the Qatar General Petroleum Company. At the launch of the re-branding, the Minister of Energy and Industry, His Excellency Abdullah bin Hamad Al Attiyah, said the new name signalled 'the transformation of QGPC from an entity struggling to find itself a place on the energy map, into a landmark of Qatar's economy and a leading corporation enjoying the confidence and respect of all local, regional and international organisations'.

QP's main subsidiaries include the following companies: (the extent of ownership by QP is given as a percentage)

National Oil Distribution Co. (NODCO) 100 per cent
Gulf Helicopters Co.(GHC) 100 per cent
Qatar Jet Fuel Co. (QATJET) 60 per cent
Qatar Fertilizer Co. (QAFCO) 75 per cent
Qatar Petrochemical Co. (QAPCO) 80 per cent
Qatar Liquefied Gas Co. (QATARGAS) 65 per cent
Ras Laffan Liquefied Natural Gas Co. (RasGas) 66.5 per cent
Qatar Fuel Additives Co. (QAFAC) 50 per cent
Qatar Vinyl Co. (QVC) 25.5 per cent
Qatar Chemical Co. (Q-CHEM) 51 per cent
Qatar Nitrogen Co. (QAN) 50 per cent.

Further downstream operations also exist within the same structures. These continue to give QP a less visible

6

but still controlling share in the operations. An example is the recently established QATOFIN, a low-density polyethylene plant owned 1 per cent by QP, 63 per cent by QAPCO (which is 80 per cent QP) and 36 per cent by Atofina; or a net ownership by QP of 51.4 per cent.

In addition, QP owns stakes in the following international operations, with the foreign partner and extent of QP's stake shown in brackets:

Arab Shipbuilding and Repair Yard (ASRY, Bahrain – QP 18.8 per cent)

Arab Maritime Petroleum Transport Co. (AMPTC, Kuwait – QP 14.8 per cent)

Arab Petroleum Investments Corp. (APICORP, Saudi Arabia – QP 10 per cent)

Arab Petroleum Services Co.
(APSC, Libya – QP 10 per cent)

Arab Petroleum Pipelines Co. (SUMED, Egypt – QP 5 per cent)

Dukhan is a thriving industrial city on the west coast of the peninsula. Oil reserves in the field are estimated at 2.2bn barrels. In the 1940s the production got under way, and Dukhan was the site of the one and only well. Today there are around 400 drilled wells along a 65-km stretch of land. These service four reservoirs. The crude oil, along with separated dry gas and condensate are pumped through a pipeline to Messaieed. Crude oil is exported from there while other products are processed to produce butane and propane. There are also gas deposits at Dukhan, which are used for feedstock and fuel.

In the 1970s, production from Dukhan was in the region of 200,000 barrels of crude oil per day. Today the field yields almost 400,000 barrels of oil, 800,000 barrels a day of gross liquid material and 330 million standard cubic feet of gas. QP's policy is to maximise production from the Dukhan field through better recovery systems and through further exploration.

Qatar's offshore production began in 1964 on the eastern seaboard – though waters in the west are also being explored. The waters are divided into six operating fields, two of which, Maydan Mazham and Bul Hanine, are operated exclusively by QP. The other four are operated through production-sharing agreements with foreign oil companies such as Maersk, Occidental and TotalFinaElf. Several exploration agreements are also in place with multinationals.

6

Gas

Natural Gas

As with the oil sector, natural gas production began as an onshore venture, associated with the Dukhan field. But in 1971 came a discovery that changed the whole thrust of Qatar's hydrocarbon strategy. A survey team found that lying just off the north-east coast was a massive gas field – the largest non-associated field ever found. The field covers more than 6,000 sq km, equivalent to almost half of Qatar's land area. It gradually became apparent that exploitation of this field would become the cornerstone of Qatar's economic activity.

The field has proven recoverable reserves of at least 600 trillion cubic feet (tcf) and its total reserves were re-estimated in May 2002 at more than 750 tcf. To put that in focus, it is more than 200 years, worth of product, not associated with oil, at the current rate of consumption. Another more realistic marker is contained in a statement made by the Finance Manager of QP in May 2002. He said that if all projects planned to be carried out in the years 2005 to 2010 go ahead, then the total reserves that used over the next 25 years would be only about 23 per cent of the new reserves figure.

The upstream exploitation of North Field gas is undertaken under a development and production sharing agreement. This agreement is a joint venture between QP and the following international companies – Total, Mobil, Mitsui and MQL. QP has a 65 per cent stake in this joint venture, Total 20 per cent, Mobil 10 per cent, Mitsui and MQL 2.5 per cent each. Exploitation of these huge resources started in 1987 with the launch of Phase 1, designed to produce gas for domestic use and a limited amount for export. Phase 2, the production of significant amounts of gas for export, got under way in 1997 with the first major exports from the Qatargas project. The focus for activities associated with the exploitation of the North Field's resources is the industrial city of Ras Laffan, located on Qatar's north-eastern shore on the southern edge of the field. The city is purpose-built to serve the gas industry.

The LNG Process

Although in many ways gas is an ideal fuel, several challenges have to be met before it can be successfully used. For Qatar, one of the main challenges is its distance from potential markets in Asia. Gas, in its raw state, is a difficult substance to transport over long distances due to its inflammability and bulk. Unlike crude oil, gas cannot simply be loaded onto a ship and transported to market. The solution to the transportation challenge lies in liquefaction. A barrel of liquefied gas is the equivalent of 600 barrels of 'gaseous' gas. Liquefied, gas is far less bulky to transport. Liquefying requires the construction of specialised facilities close to the gas field and the construction of facilities in the final market to re-gasify the gas so that it can be used as fuel. These facilities represent significant investments and therefore producers such as Qatar have to confirm long-term contracts in order to justify the construction of such facilities. Consumer countries such as Japan and South Korea must also have confidence in the long-term security of supply from gas-producing states.

After gas is extracted from the North Field, it is piped ashore to Ras Laffan. The crude natural gas that comes ashore is a mixture of chemicals, including gases such as propane and butane as well as liquids. These liquids are known as condensates, as they are gases that have condensed under the pressure of the gas field. The first stage in the liquefaction process is the separation of these condensates from the gases. In the next stage, impurities such as water, carbon dioxide and mercury are removed from the mixture. High quality gases are then separated from the remainder. These gases are then compressed and refrigerated using liquid nitrogen to achieve the very low temperatures needed to turn the gas into liquid. The result is liquefied natural gas (LNG). The equipment used in the preparation of LNG is often referred to as a train as it is a series of units linked together, like the carriages of a train. An LNG plant will often consist of more than one train and the capacity of each train is usually given in tonnes per annum, i.e. the amount of LNG capable of being produced in a year. The LNG is then stored at temperatures of around minus 160°c, before being loaded onto LNG carrier ships for transport to market. At its destination, the LNG is then returned to gaseous form before being distributed to consumers such as industry and power generators.

Qatargas

Qatargas was established in 1984 and its primary commercial activity is the operation of an LNG plant at

6

Ras Laffan and export of the product. This plant consists of three trains each with a capacity of 2 million tonnes per annum (mtpa). The last of these was completed in 1999, bringing the project up to full capacity. The LNG produced at this plant is exported to customers in Japan. The LNG production process also results in some useful by-products export. These include condensates and sulphur – both of which Qatargas exports from Ras Laffan port.

Qatargas was the first company established to take advantage of the immense opportunities that flow from Qatar's possession of extensive gas reserves. In many ways, the company has demonstrated the way forward for other Qatari companies. As well as utilising the latest technology to exploit the fuel of the future – gas – it brings together private and public sectors.

RasGas

The Ras Laffan Liquefied Natural Gas Company (RasGas) is the second of the companies formed to take commercial advantage of the country's huge gas resources. The company was formed in 1993 to operate a 5 million tonnes per annum (mtpa) LNG plant consisting of two 2.5 mtpa trains. The first of these trains became operational in the first half of 1999 and exports to Korea commenced later in that year. The second train was scheduled for completion in 2000 and exports will reach their full extent by 2003. In October 1999 the Emir of Qatar, Sheikh Hamad bin Khalifa Al Thani, officially inaugurated the $3.4 billion RasGas project.

RasGas has followed the model set out by Qatargas and is a joint venture between QP and foreign private sector companies. In 1995, the project signed a 25-year agreement with the Korea Gas Corporation (Kogas) for the supply of LNG. In addition, Kogas has an option to take a 5 per cent stake in the RasGas project. Agreements have also been signed with Indian customers for the supply of gas.

The Dolphin Project

The completion of the RasGas project marks only one step in the exploitation of Qatar's gas resources, with further plans scheduled to be implemented. The largest of these is the Dolphin project – one of the largest energy projects ever conceived. The project calls for $8-10

6

billion worth of investment over six to seven years. Unlike the Qatargas and RasGas projects, it envisages harnessing Qatari gas for regional markets. The Dolphin project proposes the construction of a pipeline from the North Field to Abu Dhabi and then on to Dubai and Oman. The gas will be used as fuel and feedstock for power generation and industries in these areas. The project may then be extended to include a submarine pipeline to Pakistan. The demand for gas in Qatar's near neighbours will grow sharply by 2005 and Qatar is uniquely positioned to satisfy this demand. Dolphin has already signed an agreement with Mobil Qatar for the supply of gas. In early 2000, Dolphin announced that TotalFinaElf and Enron had signed up as the two strategic partners along with the project's creator, the UAE Offset Group (UOG).

Petrochemicals

The origins of Qatar's petrochemical industry can be traced back to the construction of the first refinery in 1953. Refining crude oil is the most basic of petrochemical activities. The petrochemical industry really took off after 1974 when the Qatar Petrochemical Company was established. Since those early days, Qatar has established a wide range of petrochemical companies to produce chemicals from oil and gas feedstock.

These petrochemical projects combine Qatar's huge natural resources with modern technology and outside expertise to create industrial enterprises. As a result they add to the diversification of the Qatari economy and extend the range of the Emirate's exports. Bringing together the country's natural resources with modern technology also allows Qatari nationals to acquire new skills and expertise. These projects, in turn, produce chemicals that can be used as raw products in other manufacturing enterprises.

Qatar Vinyl Company (QVC)

QVC is one of Qatar's most modern enterprises and represents the developing nature of Qatar's industrial capability. QVC will use the output of Qatar's petrochemical industries to manufacture products for export and for use by other Qatari companies. QVC's operations will also encourage the creation of other companies to supply essential materials. The company was formed by Emiri decree in December 1997 following the signing of a joint venture agreement between Qatari and foreign companies.

Qatar Petrochemical Company (Qapco)

When QAPCO was formed in 1974, it was a pioneering company in more ways than one. As well as being the Emirate's first petrochemical company, it was one of the first to create a joint venture between the public and foreign private sectors. The company is a joint venture between QP (holding 80 per cent), the French company Elf Atochem (10 per cent) and the Italian company Enichem (10 per cent). The company's plant and offices are located in Messaieed, where it employs around 830 people in a 24-hour operation.

Qatar Fuel Additives Company (QAFAC)

QAFAC is one of the most modern petrochemical facilities in the country. Construction on the plant started in 1997 and when fully operational is intended to produce 825,000 metric tonnes of methanol and 610,000 tonnes of methyl tertiary-butyl ether per year. Both chemicals are added to gasoline to produce cleaner, burning fuel for automobiles. QAFAC's products are intended for export, with the first shipment leaving for India in August 1999. The plant will continue to invest in modern technology to take into account stricter environmental controls taking effect around the world.

Qatar Fertiliser Company (QAFCO)

QAFCO was formed in 1969 and its plant was the first to be constructed at the then newly-formed industrial city of Messaieed. The company has now grown into one of the world's major producers of fertiliser products. QAFCO has expanded in three distinct phases: following the completion of the initial establishment in 1974, the plant was expanded in 1979 and the third phase was completed in 1997. The fourth phase of expansion, which is presently taking place, will result in making QAFCO the largest producer of ammonia and urea in the world.

Qatar Steel Company (QASCO)

Aside from the production of crude oil, QASCO represents the oldest heavy industry enterprise in the country. The company was formed in 1975 as a joint venture between the Qatari Government and two

6

Japanese companies – Kobe Steel and Tokyo Boeki – with the Government holding 70 per cent of the company. The company's plant was completed in 1978 at Messaieed.

Qatar Nitrogen Company (QAN)

QAN is a joint venture between Qatar Industrial Manufacturing Company (QIMCO) and QP with each holding a 50 per cent stake. When fully operational, the company's plant in Messaieed will produce both gaseous and liquid nitrogen. The latter is an essential requirement in the LNG process and therefore the company will make an important contribution to the country's economic development.

Future Developments

The increase in oil production since 1995 is the result of a deliberate government policy to reinvigorate the country's oil industry and ensures that it remains a dynamic contributor to the Emirate's economic success. In order to achieve this reinvigoration and to ensure the future prosperity of the industry, QP has brought in foreign partners for their expertise and resources. The exploitation of new offshore fields at al-Rayan, al-Khaleej, al-Shaheen and al-Karkara have added production capacity. The foreign partners in these projects have included major oil companies such as Arco, Elf Aquitaine, Agip, Maersk and Occidental Petroleum. The companies are undertaking these projects under the terms of production – sharing agreements, which are typically of 25 years' length. These projects represent the future operating method for the industry – combining the best of the public and private sector interests.

Qatar is determined not to rest on its laurels and to continue searching for new oil resources. In March 1998, QP signed a five-year agreement with the US oil company Chevron for it to conduct onshore exploration. The agreement covers exploration over virtually the remainder of the peninsula outside the Dukhan field. This amounts to some 4,200 square miles (1.08 million hectares) of territory. Chevron also holds the rights to exploration of an offshore block.

6

Manufacturing

Economic diversification is one of the Government's prime economic policies and one that it has pursued with vigour. The development of manufacturing capabilities beyond the petrochemical sector is an important part of this diversification process. Although the Government has played a key role in stimulating the creation of manufacturing industries, it has also encouraged the private sector to play its full role. The result of these forward-looking economic policies is a diverse range of manufacturing companies in Qatar including **plastics, paper, chemicals** and **construction materials**. Much of this manufacturing capacity has developed since 1973, when Qatar gained the full benefit from its oil resources but the origins of manufacturing pre-date this. Manufacturing of a limited kind has probably occurred on the peninsula since its habitation – probably consisting of no more than small craft workshops and traditional boat-building enterprises using imported materials. The first modern manufacturing facility was established in 1965, when a **cement** factory was founded at Umm Bab on Qatar's western coast. Production at the factory did not actually start until 1969. After 1973, there was an explosion of manufacturing enterprises, commencing with the establishment of the **Qatar Steel Company** in 1975. These ventures continue to flourish and formulate plans for expansion, while new ventures are put into effect.

Stock Market

The establishment of the Doha Stock Market (DSM) in May 1997 marked a significant step forward in the development and expansion of financial services in the Emirate. The DSM provides exciting new investment opportunities in the Emirate and creates a new channel for Qatari companies to raise finance for expansion plans and new projects. The 35 per cent rise in the DSM index in 1998 (its first full year of operation) demonstrates the appetite for investment in stocks and shares amongst Qatari nationals. This increase made the DSM the best-performing stock exchange in the Arab world. Until early 2000, only Qatari nationals were permitted to invest in the DSM. This was extended to all Gulf Cooperation Council (GCC) nationals with cabinet approval in February 2000. Activity on the stock market slowed in 1999 as the market underwent a correction, normal after a steep rise in activity. The DSM index ended 1999 at 134.1, barely unchanged on the previous year. By early 2000, market capitalisation of the 21 companies listed on the DSM stood at just over QR18.5 billion (approximately $5.1 billion). Future plans for the DSM include relocation to purpose-built premises, the introduction of an electronic trading system and the opening of the market to non-GCC investors. These would allow the DSM to play its full role in the economic life of the Emirate.

DSM

Construction

The construction sector is set to become one of the most dynamic in the Qatari economy in the next five to ten years as the demand for new facilities, infrastructure and buildings rises. Throughout most of the 1990s, Qatar was able to commence two to three major projects annually. This represented a major impetus for the success of the sector. The continued prosperity of the sector is assured by the potential for new construction projects. This potential arises from the expansion plans noted above in the oil, gas, petrochemical and manufacturing sectors and the need to upgrade other infrastructure and buildings. Much of Qatar's infrastructure and facilities was constructed in the years immediately following 1973. It is therefore in need of upgrading and replacement. In the late 1990s, the Government embarked on major projects to upgrade the Emirate's road networks and expand Doha International Airport. In addition, Qatar's developing role as a regional and international commercial centre creates demand for the construction of new facilities.

6

Major Projects

A series of major infrastructure projects are seen as dominating the construction sector between 2002 and 2006. These projects include the following, all of which have begun:

Ras Laffan Integrated Water and Power Plant (IWPP) – one of the most exciting projects in Qatar, since it marks a new stage in the development of the country's infrastructure. The plant will be the first such integrated

IWPP

facility constructed in Qatar and, as its name suggests, will provide water and electricity for the Ras Laffan Industrial City (RLIC). The project is a joint venture called the Ras Laffan Power Company (RLPC), with the partners and their share being AES Corporation (55 per cent), QP (10 per cent), Qatar Electricity and Water Company (QEWC) (25 per cent) and Gulf Investment Corporation (GIC) (10 per cent). On completion, the power generation unit would have a capacity of 1,200 megawatts and the water plant will produce 75 million gallons a day. First power is due to be delivered in March 2003.

Dolphin – as mentioned, one of the largest energy projects ever conceived which estimates $8-10 billion investment over six to seven years. An essential element of the project is the construction of a pipeline from the North Field to Abu Dhabi and on to Dubai and Oman (and possibly eventually to Pakistan). This project was launched in 1999 and in early 2000 the strategic partners were announced.

6

Infrastructure – among these are the following (budgeted cost in: US$)

Doha International Airport Expansion ($150m)

New Doha International Airport ($500m +)

Friendship Bridge to Bahrain (feasibility study only $7m)

New Customs Centre ($67m)

Halul Harbour Upgrade ($65m)

Roads and Sewage ($200m + for the first stages)

Banking and Finance

As befits a modern and dynamic economy, Qatar possesses a sophisticated and well-regulated banking system. Qatari banks have a strong capital base, offer a wide range of services to corporate and personal customers and operate under the regulation of the Qatar Central Bank (QCB). The QCB now oversees a booming banking sector that consists of 14 commercial institutions including Qatari, foreign and Islamic banks and one specialised institution – Qatar Industrial Development Bank. The QCB was established in 1985, when it replaced the Qatar Monetary Agency, which was formed

QCB

in 1973 in the early days of Qatari independence. At the same time, the Qatari riyal was introduced as the national currency. This agency replaced an earlier currency board established in the 1960s. In 1966, the Qatar-Dubai riyal was introduced as currency to replace the Indian rupee. The modern Qatari riyal has proven a stable and reliable currency.

The banking sector in Qatar is dominated by four institutions – Qatar National Bank, Doha Bank, Commercial Bank of Qatar and al-Ahli Bank. It has shown strong growth. In 1998, profits rose by more than 25 per cent, continuing the trend of strong growth throughout much of the 1990s. The prospects for the sector look good as banks benefit from liberalisation measures introduced in the mid and late 1990s. In 1995, some restrictions on interest rates were relaxed. In 1998, almost all controls on interest rates were lifted. In addition, the QCB introduced treasury bills and bonds, which were offered for sale to Qatari banks. The move was part of the re-evaluation of the Government's monetary policy and the introduction of a more active policy on the part of the QCB. This policy should ensure that Qatar's economy and financial system retain the stability that they have long enjoyed and allow business to flourish.

6

Agriculture and Water

In Qatar, water is precious. Average annual rainfall is a mere 75mm. This falls mainly between October and March, with January the most likely month for rain. The country does, however, experience long periods with no rainfall. The Emirate has only a few underground aquifers and no surface freshwater sources. Qatar is therefore heavily reliant on desalination for its water. Two major desalination plants exist – one at Ras Abu Aboud and the other at Ras Abu Fontas. Together these supply around 17.5 billion gallons of water.

This investment in technology has allowed Qatar to develop a thriving agricultural capacity in the harsh desert conditions. In 1995, the country possessed 891 farms (compared with 338 in 1975), and this growth has allowed Qatar to become 70 per cent self-sufficient in summer vegetables and 40 per cent self-sufficient in winter vegetables. The main crops are cereals, tomatoes and other summer produce such as lettuce and cucumber, and fruits. In 1995, cereal production stood at 4,256 metric tonnes. Although this is still far short of the Emirate's needs (around 90,000 tonnes annually), it still marks a significant achievement in a country that has, historically, practised little agriculture.

Media

Al-Jazeera Television

Al-Jazeera

Since its launch in November 1996, the satellite broadcasts of Al-Jazeera Television have grown rapidly in popularity throughout the Arab world. The channel was established by a group of Qatari business executives supported by a government loan. The collapse of the BBC's Arabic-language satellite television earlier in the year provided a pool of talented journalists and production staff that the new station could exploit and combine with the excellent broadcasting facilities that already existed in the Emirate.

Al Jazeera is known throughout the world for its role in airing the Osama Bin Laden videos. This does not spring from any Islamic fundamentalist alliance, but from a remarkably resilient policy of editorial independence and freedom, which frequently upsets its sensitive neighbours.

Al Jazeera refuses to give in to diplomatic pressure. This is a completely new phenomenon in the Arab world, where heavy state control of all media is an established way of life.

Telecommunications

The infrastructure built by the Qatar Telecommunications company (Q-Tel) for business and domestic users now boasts some 350,000 telephone landlines and 70,000 mobile telephone lines. The latter are compatible with the global standard for mobiles (GSM). This network provides modern communications throughout the country and integrates Qatar into the global communications system. Early in the 21st century, Qatar will have become directly connected to the fibre-optic cable known as Flag, linking Europe with Japan via the Gulf.

Communications

Qatar has developed a modern and sophisticated communications infrastructure to serve its fast-growing economy. In keeping with its commitment to trade, the Emirate has constructed an integrated network for the import and export of goods and their distribution around the country. A reliable telecommunications network supports its communications infrastructure and allows business to use the latest technology to run operations. Qatari businesses and other organisations, like their counterparts elsewhere, are developing a strong presence on the Internet.

Qatar has over 1,100 km of paved road, with the network centred naturally on the capital, Doha. Well-maintained dual carriageways link Doha with al-Ruwais on the northern tip of the peninsula, Dukhan in the west, Abu Samrah and Sawda Natheel in the south on the border with Saudi Arabia, and of course with the port of Messaieed, south of Doha. In addition, the dual carriageways to Abu Samrah and Sawda Natheel integrate Qatar into the regional road network – linking the country with Saudi Arabia and the UAE.

The completion of a new terminal at Doha International Airport early in the 21st century will have enhanced Qatar's already first-class air services and make a significant contribution to the Emirate's economic development. Qatar is an ideal transit point between Europe and North America on one hand, and Asia on the other. Additionally, it will provide a conveniently-located entry point for the Gulf region. Over 20 international airlines already serve Doha, linking Qatar to virtually every major business centre on every continent, often on a daily basis.

6

Tourism

Qatar's tourism industry is growing in leaps and bounds. It was in 1989 that Qatar recognised its rich potential for tourism, and has been developing this sector ever since. The Qatar General Tourist Authority (GTE) was created in 2000, with aims of further developing and coordinating the industry. In 2000, Qatar had only 480,000 visitors classed as tourists and accounted their value to the economy as 0.48 per cent of GDP, which was the lowest of all the GCC countries. With the renewed focus on tourism led by the GTA and new foreign investment laws allowing foreigners to own up to 100 per cent in tourism projects and the right to lease land for up to 50 years, this is truly a growth area. New hotels, new leisure facilities and events, both cultural and sporting, will all contribute to the growth, which is targeted to increase four-fold within the next two years.

March 2002 saw the opening of the Qatar Airways and Holiday Centre, equipped with VIP suites and Internet access, among other tourist comforts. The Centre was funded by Qatar Airways Leisure, which comprises the inward-bound destination company Discover Qatar; and outward-bound tour operator Qatar Airways Holidays.

Qatar is becoming known for its expertise in staging international events. The Emirate enjoys excellent links to all corners of the world, international class hotels and top class exhibition, conference and sporting facilities. These facilities include hotels such as the Sheraton (the first international class hotel in Doha, opened in 1982) and Marriott. Qatar also boasts a premier exhibition and conference centre in the Qatar International Exhibition Centre (QIEC) in the West Bay area of Doha, covering 10,000 square metres. The QIEC regularly hosts business and trade exhibitions that attract executives from around the globe.

International Events

The country has become the preferred location for international and regional political, business and sporting events. These events provide important opportunities for Qatar to demonstrate the dynamism of its economy, the stability of its political and social environments and the excellence of its business infrastructure. Qatar has hosted major political and business events, such as the 1997 Middle East and North Africa Conference – a gathering of regional and international political and business leaders that played an important role in supporting the Arab-Israeli peace process. The decision to hold the conference in Doha was a reflection of the good relations that Qatar enjoys with all states in the region. Other important regional summits held in Doha include the Organisation of Islamic Conference (OIC) Foreign Ministers Meeting in March 1998 and OIC and the Gulf Cooperation Council, Heads of State Summit in 1997.

7

establishing a presence in Qatar

establishing a presence in Qatar

The aim of this section is to
provide a sweeping overview for
the visitor who is considering
the possibility of a local office.
Here are some of the pitfalls
and benefits, an insight into the
legal situation, and some of the
major issues to be considered,
such as recruiting, finding
premises, etc.

This chapter will briefly examine some of the pros and cons of setting up a local operation. For some activities, such as contracting, there is just no other way to do business. In others, such as the professional services, it is sometimes the case that a local partner needs to be taken on board to be able to register.

Whatever your situation, the best advice is (as always) to seek professional advice to guide you through the labyrinth of legalities and procedures. Take this advice early, before you start spinning your wheels in the wrong direction.

Your agent/sponsor/distributor/intended partner will be able to help and will almost certainly be happy to explain the intricacies of the options and procedures. But be cautious. He may know of other options suited to your business but prefer and push you towards a particular approach because it suits his overall business activities. He may well recommend suitable legal and financial counsel, but check others and make your own mind up which service provider you are comfortable with. Most would be happy for you to get a second opinion. If your intended partner or sponsor does get seriously upset because you don't trust his advice, then you will maybe want to reconsider the arrangement and his suitability.

The Benefits of being 'Local'

These are many and varied but in all probability the prime benefit is that, unless you are present and are willing to trade as a local operation, your chances of success will be limited. Qatar is a welcoming place, rich in material wealth, and wants to use that resource to develop all aspects of the country. A project that utilises and adds value to the natural resources, creates jobs, generates other industries and provides training and growth for the local population will be well received. Such a project will also be well rewarded with substantial investment incentives to the joint venture operations such as:

- Natural gas priced at US$0.6 to 0.75 per million British thermal unit.
- Electricity at US$0,0178 per kWh
- Industrial land at a nominal rent of one Qatari riyal

(US$0.28) per square metre per year
- No customs duties on imports of machinery, equipment and spare parts required for the project
- No export duties
- No taxes on corporate profits for pre-determined periods
- No personal income taxes
- No exchange controls regulations.

A Welcome to Investors

Despite its natural wealth from the income produced by oil and gas, Qatar still has a very clear view of the need for foreign investment. It has forward-thinking policies to encourage foreign companies to share their skills and knowledge in return for fair compensation by way of protecting a return on their investment. Economic liberalisation measures have been introduced to encourage inward investment, particularly in the private sector.

In developing these policies the Minister of Finance, Economy and Commerce has been given wide powers to increase the percentage of foreign ownership beyond the maximum figure stated in the Law. This is, of course, subject to considerable scrutiny and depends on the perceived value to the country in making such concessions.

The Legal Framework

There are two laws that have a bearing on establishing a business in Qatar:

Foreign Investments Law

The Foreign Investments Law No.13 of 2000, came into force on 25 November 2000 and replaced Law No.25 of 1990. Under this law there are essentially four ways in which a foreign (non-Qatari) commercial or services business may establish itself directly:

- **Local Joint Venture Company**
This is the famous 51/49 per cent arrangement where the local (Qatari) partner must hold a minimum of 51 per cent of the shares in the business. These are quite workable and probably the most common way in which foreign companies arrange themselves with a local operation. Of course, with the ownership also goes the profit as well as control of the business; or so it would

seem on paper. Loss of control is seldom an issue. The foreign partner, to all intents and purposes, runs the business. The local partner contributes with administration and support in the market and *majlis* (meetings). As to profits, the simple question to be asked is, do you want 49 per cent of something or 100 per cent of nothing?

● **Branch of a Foreign Company**
A foreign company may, by Ministerial Decree (through the Ministry of Finance, Economy and Trade), establish a branch in Qatar to invest monies for economic development purposes, to facilitate the performance of a public service or to achieve a public utility in selected fields – industrial, agricultural, tourism, etc. Such companies are also allowed to import goods for the furtherance of such activity provided no suitable local goods exist. A Qatari agent needs to be appointed to carry out the arrangements for visas and permits associated with the work of the branch – such organisations are usually only put in place for a specific project and are wound up at the end of that project.

● **Branch of an Existing Qatari Company**
This is commonly used where the Qatari company establishes a division or branch within its existing Commercial Registration. The arrangement is controlled by a management agreement between the parties, whereby the foreign company runs the business (usually in all senses of the word including full risk to profit and loss) and the local company takes an agreed sponsorship fee and a commission on results. The disadvantage is that the foreign company risks losing its name (it is registered as a part of the local company) and the business is open to attack as not truly being a local entity, commercially or legally.

● **Supply of Manpower, Technical Equipment and Services**
Utilising Article 12 of the Foreign Investments Law, it is possible to avoid local incorporation if one claims compliance with this article.

Commercial Companies Law
In establishing a local presence, there are clear and unequivocal procedures which govern the setting up of business operations in Qatar, all of which have their

basis in Commercial Companies Law No.5 of 2002, which in June of that year replaced law No.11 of 1981. At the time of writing, the Law had just been changed and the details were being absorbed by the legal profession and businesses. There seems to be little change in the possible structures although the detail of permissible limits of ownership and responsibility will have been revised. Some of these are:

- The restrictions on non-Qatari shareholders in public limited companies is amended to allow a percentage limit for foreign shareholders.
- The introduction of a bankruptcy law.
- The creation of a register of company charges, and legislature relating to priority of registered charges.
- The agencies, trademarks and intellectual property regulations.

Obviously there has been little opportunity for the law to be tested in the courts and it is especially advisable to get good, qualified, legal advice.

The Basic Structures

Joint Liability Company

- A Joint Liability Company is one consisting of two or more partners whereby the partners are personally and jointly responsible for the company's obligations.
- The name of the company shall be in the names of all partners, or the name of one partner followed by the words 'and partners'.
- A Joint Liability Company may be administered by all partners unless otherwise agreed.

Partnership in Commendam

- A Partnership in Commendam refers to a company consisting of two types of partners:
- Simple partners who are empowered to administer the affairs of the company and are jointly and personally responsible for the company's obligations.
- Commendite (sleeping) partners, merely contributing to the company's capital without being responsible for its obligations except to the value of their shares in the capital.

Limited Partnership in Shares

A Limited Partnership in Shares refers to a company consisting of one or more simple partners (personally responsible for the company's obligations) and a number of shareholding partners, which shall be not less than 10 in number:

• A Limited Partnership in Shares must have a capital of at least 200,000 Qatari riyals and is managed by one or more simple partners.

Limited Liability Company

• A Limited Liability Company (LLC) derives its name from the partners' limited liability towards the company's obligations. A limited liability company must have at least two partners and not more than 30.

• It must have a minimum capital of 200,000 Qatari riyals.

• The capital must be fully subscribed before registration.

• The management of the company is conducted by one or more managers whether they are partners in the company or not.

• A manager in an LLC may not take a managerial post in any similar or competitive company, or conduct similar business for his personal account or for the account of others unless approved by the company's general assembly.

• An LLC with a capital exceeding 500,000 Qatari riyals must appoint one or more auditors.

• An LLC may not engage in the business of insurance, banking or investment of funds on behalf of others.

Shareholding Company

A shareholding company consists of an unlimited number of shareholders and must be registered with a name derived from its objectives.

• Partners must be Qatari nationals except in the following cases:

if the partners are nationals of Arab Countries, provided that in accordance with any bilateral treaties, the principle of reciprocity exists

if there is a need for the investment of foreign capital or foreign expertise, provided the approval of the Minister of Finance, Economy and Commerce is obtained.

• For the purposes of encouraging privatisation, the law allows the government to establish one or more shareholding companies, whether alone or with others, whether or not nationals or foreigners and whether or not natural or judicial.

7

115

● Articles of Association and bye-laws of every shareholding company must be published in the official gazette upon its incorporation and registration.

● The company's capital must be not less than 500,000 Qatari riyals

● The company should be administered by a board of directors consisting of not fewer than five members and not more than 11 members. The term of office for directors shall be not more than three years but may be extended.

● The ordinary General Assembly is vested with the power to elect the board of directors.

● Some matters, such as increase or decrease of capital of the company, its merger with any other company or companies, where in the latter case the company shall cease to exist, will be dealt with at an Extraordinary General Assembly.

Taxation

Taxation is covered by Law No.11 of 1993. In general the law provides that any business activity carried out in Qatar will be subject to tax. Income tax is levied on partnerships and companies operating in Qatar whether they operate through branches or in partnerships with foreign companies.

Tax is not levied on Qatari owned business enterprise. Law No.9 of 1989 provides that nationals of the GCC states be treated as Qatari citizens for income tax purposes and thus pay no income tax. There are no personal income taxes, social insurance or other statutory deductions from salaries and wages paid to individuals in Qatar.

Administration

Qatar uses the Gregorian calendar for income tax purposes but there is no specific tax year. Taxpayers may apply to prepare financial statements for any twelve-month period ending on any day as long as that day is not 31 December.

Tax declarations must be filed within four months of the end of the company's financial period. This deadline may be extended at the discretion of the Department of Taxation in The Ministry of Finance, Economy and Commerce but may not exceed in any case eight months. Penalties exist for late filing or failure to submit tax returns. These can be onerous and attention to the requirements and the advice of your accountants and auditors should be treated seriously.

Determination

Tax liabilities are computed in a manner generally similar to the British and American practices, that is, on the basis of profits disclosed by audited financial statements, adjustments for tax depreciation and any items allowed as not taxable by the Income Tax Department.

Generally, Capital Gains arising from the sale of business assets and business interests are included as an ordinary income, as are the aggregate of all gains and profits that are realised or have arisen from carrying out the business activity in Qatar.

While the tax payer is required to declare the full value of a supply and installation contract, the value of supply and other engineering services performed outside the country are normally (given the existence of valid documentary evidence) allowed as a cost in the income statement.

7

Tax rates

Currently these start at nil on profits up to 100,000 Qatari riyals. Above that, tax starts at the rate of 10 per cent for profits between 100 and 500,000 and then increase in additional tolls of 5 per cent for each additional 500,000. The maximum level is 35 per cent, which is due on profits of more than 5 million Qatari riyals.

Accounting principles

Generally accepted methods of commercial accounting must be applied and the accruals method must be followed. If a taxpayer wishes to use a different accounting method, prior approval of the tax administration must be obtained. Compliance with International Accounting Standards is recommended.

Tax treaties

Qatar has signed double taxation treaties with Algeria, Bangladesh, France, India, Morocco, Romania, Russia, Senegal and Tunisia. Some countries, including the UK, USA and Japan, allow some unilateral relief against their own taxes for income tax paid in Qatar.

No taxes

Presently there is no personal tax, sales tax, value-added tax, estate tax, or gift tax levied in Qatar.

Other Considerations

There are many aspects of embarking on an overseas venture that cannot be simplified in a few phrases in a guide-book. Detailed knowledge and understanding are essential and the best advice (again) is to get a professional advise you. This section aims to provide some general points to consider and review on the personnel front.

Workforce

With such a small indigenous population, there are few opportunities to employ nationals although there is, quite rightly, a strong push to get the younger generation trained and in work. This is called Qatarisation. Generally speaking, the work force is multi-national and multi-cultural and is made up mainly from the Indian sub-continent and the Arab world. Skills and abilities are variable and immigration rules, based on a desire to manage a balanced spread of nationalities, often means visa and residence permits for the people you want are not readily available.

The employer/sponsor is essentially responsible for all aspects of the individual's arrival, stay and departure from the country. This means you need to get to grips with a whole host of non-work related issues, such as housing, health and transport to and from the place of work. This responsibility is not confined to the lower-level worker; it applies equally to all levels and all nationalities.

Salaries

There is little that cannot be solved with some thought and effort, but it all takes time and perhaps a loss of focus on what you came for in the first place.

Many Western expatriates are willing to work for a tax-free wage that is no longer a multiple of their gross salary at home. But remember to add on the additional costs of airfares, housing, utilities, telephones, schooling, local transport, medical care, end of service gratuity, etc. These easily add up to another salary per person.

Housing

A full range of possibilities for housing exists, from super luxurious compounds which are more like five-star resorts with all the trimmings (and prices to match), to more simple compounds and individual houses, right down to basic room or flat sharing. Bachelors tend to be housed in company camps with several to a room, or dormitory, with bunk beds and common messing. For the newcomer, space can often be found for the first batch of workers in an established company's camp.

Rents range from a few hundred to thousands of Qatari riyals per month. What you spend depends on your needs and staff profile. There are several good estate agents more than willing to help. Letting and lease arrangements are usually handled by them (for which the landlord pays) and one can pay per month (often with post-dated cheques).

Medical care

Medical facilities are many, inexpensive and of a high standard. Make sure that you provide all your staff with a local medical card, which costs only QR100. Western expatriates will probably expect private medical cover with medical repatriation costs covered as well.

7

Time

Whatever you do allow for plenty of time. The old adage that 'time is money', holds so true. Things won't go smoothly. Consider the scenario: your senior resident manager has a minor traffic accident. He is prevented from working because he has to wait for a traffic cop to appear, then make a personal appearance at a police station across town to handle the paperwork. Your middle management are diverted from their duties to help resolve the matter, because the papers are not in order and your manager must wait until papers are delivered. Your unsupervised workforce slows down, your output plummets. It's all quite possible!

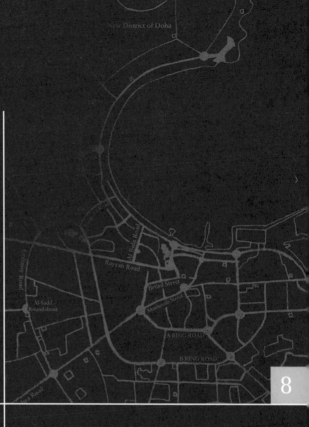

8

where to stay, and what to eat

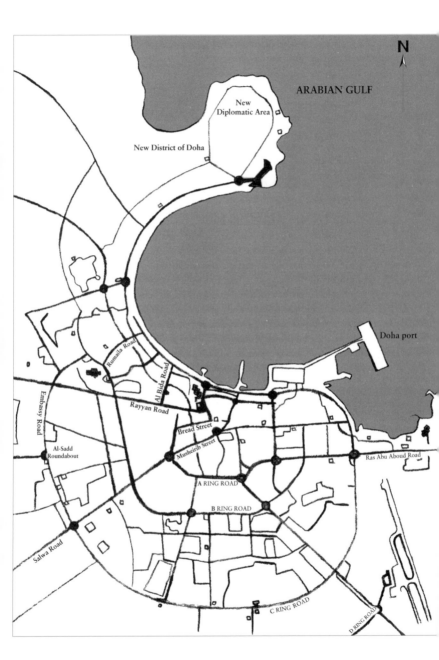

N

ARABIAN GULF

New
Diplomatic Area

New District of Doha

Doha port

Rumaila Road

Al Bida Road

Rayyan Road

Embassy Road

Bread Street

Musheirib Street

Al-Sadd
Roundabout

Ras Abu Aboud Road

A RING ROAD

B RING ROAD

Salwa Road

C RING ROAD

D RING ROAD

Doha

Hotels in Doha

The West Bay is actually north of the city – and these days it is not really a bay at all, having had an enormous amount of new land reclaimed from the shallow sea to make room for the marinas and beaches which are springing up. The West Bay is where all the spanking new five-star luxury hotels, resorts, recreational facilities and conference centres are being sited. Smaller, although no less modern in facilities and amenities, business hotels are also on the rise in the more traditional downtown areas.

There is now a good – and growing – range of quality hotel accommodation in Doha. Prominent in the West Bay was the Hotel Inter-Continental Doha which opened in late 2000 – the first new five-star hotel to be built for several years. This was a significant development, as it offered, literally, concrete evidence of the anticipated growth in trade that would flow from the successful marketing of Qatar's LNG. It was soon followed in 2001 by the Ritz-Carlton, a little further along the new West Bay development. These two hotels will form the keystones of the West Bay project – the next major phase of Doha's growth. Construction of the Four Seasons Hotel complex (adjacent to the Sheraton) is well advanced.

As examples of the business hotel category the Mövenpick, adjacent to the Corniche, also opened in late 2001 and the Holiday Inn is going through its fit-out to be open and in business by the time this book is published.

All of the older hotels have been refurbished, or are in the process of being so. More rooms in all categories are planned. Gone are the days of being thrown out of your hotel to make way for a major conference or sleeping on cruise ships for lack of hotel space (although that was rather fun).

Hotel Inter-Continental Doha
❑ Tel: 484 4444; fax: 483 9555
This is everything you would expect from the five-star Inter-Continental chain. Their long experience in and of the Gulf is evident in the design of the newly-opened hotel and its many amenities, which are designed to cater equally to business travellers and tourists (Internet

8

123

connection in every room). The hotel is in what is described as 'the up and coming' area of West Bay, meaning the government has big plans for this quarter, although currently the hotel stands alone in its own grounds with no near neighbours. Rooms are large, elegant and beautifully appointed and the public areas are suitably grand and Arabesque. It will be a pleasure to watch the property mature as time goes by.

Most guests come to relax, and this is when the Inter-Continental really comes into its own, with a decent-sized outdoor pool and beach, and a good choice of water sports and other activities. The pool is chilled in summer and heated in winter. At ? km long, the wide sandy beach with its distinctive blue-and-white striped umbrellas and chairs is a great place to spend the day. Water sports options, which can be used even by non-hotel guests, include diving, water-skiing, banana boats, parasailing, windsurfing and fishing, all run by professional staff, while the list of land-based sports equally impressive, with tennis, squash, table-tennis, beach volleyball and an enviable gym with views overlooking the pool. The children's paddling pool and play areas are covered to protect the little ones from the sun. A variety of snacks, meals and drinks are available through the pool bar, and waiter service is available at both the pool and on the beach, although during busy times you'll find it's quicker to order at the outdoor Pool Terrace restaurant.

The Ritz Carlton
❑ Tel: 484 8000; fax: 484 8484

The elegant blue-and-sand colours of the Ritz-Carlton's twenty-two storey tower on the edge of West Bay is delivering all that was promised. Opened eventually in late 2001 in time for the World Trade Conference, the hotel and its Marina have certainly joined The Doha Sheraton at the top of the list in terms of size and opulence. Both are owned by the government-owned Qatar National Hotels, and give a lie to the old adage that one can't run a service industry with a civil service. The internal décor is amazing, with the Atrium going all the way to the top of its 22 stories. The lobby is enormous and delightful to sit in and drink afternoon tea to the strains of live music. The restaurants and function rooms are artfully hidden, and while it can be a bit of a struggle for first-time visitors to locate their destination, the abundance of well-informed, friendly and helpful staff make short work of any difficulties. Ritz-Carlton's operations have become synonymous with elegance and luxury, combined with business efficiency and their Doha property looks set to maintain those standards. Rooms are plush and spacious with gold and blue the dominant colours, and almost all face the waters of the Gulf. All the usual five-star extras apply. Excellent and varied dining options (see below). The Ritz-Carlton Doha is set to be the place to see and be seen.

The Sheraton Doha Hotel & Resort
❏ Tel: 485 4444; fax: 483 2323

Originally built in time for a major Arab conference, the triangular, futuristic Sheraton Doha stands proud at one end of the Corniche. Located near to the diplomatic area, on the Corniche which houses the head offices of the major industries, and at the start of the connections to the West Bay, and the new highway to Ras Laffan and the north, it remains a popular place for functions. The hotel is currently undergoing comprehensive refurbishment and upgrading, but this is being skilfully managed to avoid disruption. The hotel's public areas are impressive and modern-Arabesque in style and the rooms large and elegant. This, coupled with excellent sports and leisure facilities on-site, will ensure that the Sheraton maintains its share of the tourist trade. The country's Exhibition Centre is across the road and the Conference Centre within the complex has already been used for a number of extremely high-profile events, such as the World Trade Conference in late 2001.

The Doha Marriott Gulf Hotel
❏ Tel: +974 429 8888; fax: +974 441 8784

Previously the Gulf Sheraton, The Doha Marriott Gulf Hotel has had a complete overhaul. This makes it an excellent business hotel, recognised as a deluxe beachfront hotel on the eastern side of Doha Bay, with breathtaking views of the hotel's marina, private beach, Qatar's capital city and its Corniche. Centrally located, it is five minute's drive from Doha International Airport. The usual Marriott efficiency and strength of service is much in evidence, as are first-class leisure facilities. The new spa at The Marriott has the finest treatments in

8

town, together with a state-of-the-art fitness centre to mix business with pleasure. The spa offers a new dimension in fitness and relaxation in the country. The health clinic has a wide range of beauty treatments and natural remedies. There are two floodlit outdoor tennis courts, temperature-controlled outdoor pool, private beach, children's pool, private marina, jacuzzi, and water-skiing. Business needs are not forgotten. The Concierge Lounge in the Doha Marriott Tower has been designed to offer business travellers the most modern, efficient and comfortable working environment. The Marriott is also fully equipped to stage conventions, conferences, banquets and receptions of any scale or type via its fine range of conference, ballrooms and banqueting rooms with attendant salons and annexes, plus an Executive Lounge on the rooftop.

The Ramada Hotel
❑ Tel: 441 7417; fax: 4410941

A stalwart of the business hotel scene since the late 1970s, the Ramada scores heavily for its (nearly) downtown location. It also seems to be a magnet for the expatriate community, many of whom have grown up with the Ramada over the years. However that should in no way deter the new visitor. Superbly located on the C Ring Road at Ramada Junction (where else, and for the old hands for 'junction' read 'roundabout'), Ramada is central for everywhere. Turn right on the Salwa Road to go to the old downtown areas; turn left and take the Salwa Road to the Industrial Estates and the border crossing to Saudi Arabia. Left at the ring road takes you to the airport, and right to Al Sadd and West Bay. The guest-rooms, gardens and fitness facilities have been refurbished and upgraded recently. For business visitors, the Ramada is possibly the best value in town.

The Sofitel Doha Palace Hotel
❑ Tel: 443 5222; fax: 443 9186

Having undergone something of an overdue overhaul and upgrade, the Sofitel now offers good quality and good value accommodation in the heart of Doha. The coffee shop is conveniently located off the lobby on the mezzanine floor. It offers a good buffet lunch while the other food and beverage outlets at the top of the building have some of the best views around, many of them

8

overlooking the *suq* area which is highly atmospheric at night. That location, in the heart of the *suq*, does not bode well for access by car and/or for easy street parking. However, the Sofitel does have an underground carpark. The French influence pervades – which is good news for foodies.

The Oasis Hotel and Beach Club
❑ Tel: 442 4424; fax: 432 7096

Probably the oldest of the better hotels. No longer five star, but certainly still an option for the business visitor on a smaller budget. The decent-sized rooms have recently been refurbished and the beach club is as good as anywhere in town. Good location near the airport, popular with flight crews and people who need access to Qatar Petroleum and early departures to offshore locations.

The Mövenpick Hotel Doha
❑ Tel: 429 1111; fax: 429 1100

The Mövenpick Hotel also opened late 2001 to cater for the demands for rooms brought about by the Doha Round of the World Trade Conference. Another in the Qatar National Hotel's stable, this property is located just off the Corniche and near to the National Museum. The airport is a five-minute drive away. Fully equipped with the usual amenities expected of a business hotel, the main restaurant combines the various different culinary styles with the décor. Easy taking a guest; no need to change restaurant if you decide you really wanted an American steak instead of Chinese noodles! Because the original design was as a residence for older folk, the corridors are very wide and have many ramps. It has a health club and spa, swimming pool, business centre, and three sound-proofed suites, which can be combined to make a small seminar and banquet centre, complete the offering.

Coming Soon

By the time this guide is in print the following hotels will be open for business:

The Holiday Inn
The Holiday Inn will be up and running on the Rayan Road at Mannai Roundabout, easy for access to the

8

downtown *suq* areas, and to the business areas, particularly the banking industry's head offices. This hotel will prove a welcome addition to Doha's business hotels. Like the Hotel Inter-Continental Doha, it is part of the Six Continents Group and expects to provide the service for which its management is renowned.

Rydges Plaza Hotel
Another property superbly located adjacent to the Corniche, which is set for opening before the end of 2002. An attractive modern structure, which, as it nears completion on the outside, has already become a significant landmark on the skyline. The services promised from this 136-room property housed in eleven stories includes the usual things one would expect from a business hotel. An all-day dining 'Garden Courtyard' style of restaurant should be a first in Doha.

Hotel Restaurants

These are listed separately since the variety now offered by the hotel outlets is enormous. Barring something really unusual like Alaskan Inuit, I would challenge any visitor not to be able to find the type of food he or she prefers in Doha. If you cannot find it in a hotel you will almost certainly find it outside, of which more below. The second reason is that alcohol is only available in hotel-based outlets or clubs. Public restaurants are not granted alcohol licences. If, for you, a meal is not complete without wine, beer or spirits then read no further than these paragraphs.

Most of the hotels also provide an excellent outside catering service (as do restaurants). The most popular were, and it seems still are, the Ramada and the Doha Sheraton & Resort Hotel. None of this will be of particular interest to the visitor, but may explain why, if during an extended visit, they are entertained at several different homes and served off the same plates by the same staff!

French/Mediterranean

La Mer (Ritz-Carlton)
With a head for heights one has a wonderful view from 23 floors up! The hotel's opulent signature restaurant offers innovative Lebanese cuisine with a modern interpretation of Middle Eastern recipes.

La Villa (Sofitel)
Cosy new restaurant on the 12th floor of the Sofitel. Only 56 covers and a nice homely feel. High quality Mediterranean cooking.

La Brasserie (Sofitel)
French café-style restaurant and very popular for business lunches. Classic French dishes plus some other delicacies from around the world. Excellent buffet lunch menu. Usual high Sofitel standards.

Maxim (Ramada)
One of the contenders for best dining in town, Maxim offers up-market French cuisine, beautifully prepared and served. It has a warm and almost rustic atmosphere and the food is fabulously rich and rewarding. Make sure you book, because the restaurant is a popular choice for spoiling business clients and for family celebrations and treats.

Al Shaheen (Sheraton Doha)
Rooftop restaurant offering elegant French cuisine with some Italian pasta overtones and tremendous views over the city and the Corniche. Great fish dishes. Very smart fixtures and fittings – great for a special night out. If you have a large party to entertain, there are a couple of private rooms adjacent to the main restaurant where it's possible to entertain in grand style.

8

Italian
Cielo (Hotel Inter-Continental Doha)
Even without the food, Cielo recreates the atmosphere of sitting outside in a typical Italian town square, with tables set underneath stripy awnings. The ceiling has been painted to look like the afternoon sky, complete with rooftops and fluffy clouds (Cielo is Italian for 'sky'). The perspective of the painted buildings moves as you walk around, giving the impression that they are three-dimensional. In the kitchen, Chef Salvatore Coco – from Sicily – cooks classic Italian cuisine. Cielo is the genuine article, with a surprisingly wide choice of dishes and tastes. Definitely worth a visit.

La Veranda (Sheraton Doha)
After a hard work-out at the adjacent sports and fitness club, why not undo all that effort by having a splendid Italian meal at La Veranda? There is an excellent salad buffet to accompany your selection of dishes and Chef

Leonardo Concezzi, from the heart of Italy, has created mouthwatering menus. Great views of the Gulf and Corniche and a choice of inside/outside dining.

Italian Job (Ramada)

Probably the most popular restaurant in town. The name comes from the film starring Michael Caine, and many original photos from the film adorn the walls. The menu covers everything from a freshly-made pizza to a full traditional Italian dinner, with home-made pasta dishes cooked in the open kitchen for all to see. Booking in advance is highly recommended, unlike a sense of humour, which according to a sign at the entrance is obligatory to gain access.

Porcini (Ritz-Carlton)

Renaissance décor with the emphasis on intimate and romantic dining. The menu reflects a range of Italian regional cooking with terrific freshly-baked breads. Open kitchen and food preparation at table makes you part of the action. One of the newer venues but developing a reputation for excellence.

8

Tex-Mex

Paloma (Hotel Inter-Continental Doha)

The theme in Paloma is that of a rustic hacienda in Mexico, with dark wooden beams and plaster walls. Traditional Mexican and Native-American items decorate the walls. The food on the menu echoes this, offering a selection of Mexican and hearty Texan dishes. Swapping a traditional chef's hat for a stylish bandana, Chef Pablo Flores (from Mexico) oversees the open-plan kitchen. Those who believe that Mexican food consists of only refried beans will be pleasantly surprised by the variety of dishes on offer, from cheesy *quesadillas* to the traditional *tacos*, *nachos* and *tortillas*. The atmosphere in the restaurant is helped along by the live Latin-American band, followed by the DJ who takes over the dance floor at 11pm. Definitely the liveliest venue in town at weekends.

Salsa (Doha Marriott)

Through the swinging saloon doors of Salsa, you are transported to a colourful Mexican courtyard. Salsa provides an à la carte menu of Tex-Mex favourites accompanied by live (loud) music and, in between sets, a (loud) parrot. Enjoy *fajitas*, *burritos*, three-alarm chilli and *enchiladas*, along with steaks served on sizzling platters. Quench your thirst with ice-cold Coronas or frozen Margaritas in this robust *plazita* while enjoying the atmosphere.

Asian/oriental/fusion

Chingari (Ramada)

Excellent Indian restaurant with stylish décor and decoration. This is a typical Tandoori Indian Restaurant presented in relaxing and stylish décor. An extensive menu specializing in dishes cooked in Tandoori ovens, after marinating in herbs and spices. The wide variety of breads complement meals. The staff are happy to help you order the right combinations. Live Indian music is provided most nights. Beware the Indian beer denoted 'strong' on the drinks list. 'Lethal but wonderful' would be a better description. Food is prepared to order and service is accordingly slow. Go with a group of good conversationalists and be prepared to switch off the mobile and chill out for a while.

Taj Rasoi (Doha Marriott)

Elegant, rich and sophisticated, Taj Rasoi represents the best of India. A combination of deep mahogany wood carvings and an opulent marble-trimmed floor give this room an aura of the golden period of India.

Tandoori ovens and the kitchen open on to the dining room (protected by a glass divider), allowing the chefs to become part of the dining experience as they prepare fresh *naans*, *parata*, *kulcha* and tandoori grills. (Note, this restaurant is alcohol free.)

Asia Live! (Doha Marriott)

Incorporating design elements of Thailand, Japan and China, including intricately carved wooden structures, bamboo furnishings and lacquered finishings, the restaurant brings the beauty of the Far East to Doha. Focusing primarily on Japanese, Chinese and Thai cuisine, it features the best of each country. The kitchen has a Chinese cooking range and a special oven for the preparation of Peking duck. Inside the dining room, two *tepanyaki* tables allow guests to enjoy delicious grilled steaks and seafood as skilled chefs entertain them by preparing their dinners before them. Elegant and simple, the focus is on service, food and presentation. Finally, an in-room *sushi* counter will serve guests throughout the restaurant.

8

Sakura (Ramada)
Ramada has a brand new outlet offering Japanese cuisine, complementing its other choices of eating outlets. Specialising in *tepanyaki* and *shushi*, with two private dining rooms, it is ideal for groups of eight to ten. Very popular with the local Japanese expatriate community as well as Europeans and Americans.

Fish

Doha has an excellent array of locally-caught fish and shellfish. Most of the restaurants in town will feature local produce and the fish market itself is well worth a visit, just to see the range and quality on offer.

Sultan Ibrahim (Hotel Inter-Continental Doha)
If you love fish and yet pine for the flavours of Middle Eastern cooking, this is the ideal spot. Beautifully situated where the hotel's manicured grounds meet the Gulf, Sultan Ibrahim offers fabulous local *hammour* (white fish), Gulf prawns and their like, complemented by Lebanese cooking. Diners select their fish from the display, which is then weighed and prepared how you like by Chef Jean Makhoul. Beware of 'eating with your eyes' as both the fish and vegetables are paid for by the 100g – take the staff's advice when in doubt about how much to order. The introduction of a belly dancer and band has added to its popularity with the locals as well as visitors, so book early to avoid disappointment.

Captain's Grill (Ritz-Carlton)
Built out over the marina and decorated in a suitably nautical style, the Captain's Grill offers a sumptuous selection of local fish. Live lobsters in a tank do their best to look small and unappetising, but fail miserably. Informal fishy snacks are to be had in the adjacent bar.

Coffee Shops and Others

Al Waleema (Ritz-Carlton)
All day coffee-shop dining in bright and pleasant surroundings. 40-foot high windows offer views over the gardens and the Gulf. Buffet style much in evidence.

Laffan (Sheraton Doha)
Situated on the hotel's mezzanine floor and brightly decorated, the Laffan features a style of cooking they call 'Asia de Cuba'. This is fusion cooking, with the fused elements being Asian, Cuban and Caribbean flavours. A

wild array of possibilities here – some genuinely original, others perhaps a bit ambitious. But anything with 'Cuba' in the name is in vogue at the moment and Cuba's excellent tobacco products are available.

Al Hubara (Sheraton Doha)
One floor down is the lobby-level coffee shop with what has become the standard Gulf breakfast, lunch and dinner buffet. Al Hubara rings the changes by having a different theme each day of the week, and for those with an appetite, this is the kind of place for you.

Hyde Park (Ramada)
Full buffet for breakfast, lunch and dinner as well as an à la carte menu. Everything is available from a quick snack to a full meal. Friday brunch is a popular meeting point for the local community and offers excellent value for a varied and wide choice of different cuisine.

Breezes (Ritz Carlton)
Light food, casual and relaxed atmosphere. Overlooks the Gulf and has a delightful patio area. Burgers, sandwiches, snacks.

8

Pirates' Cove (Sheraton Doha)
Outdoor dining on a wharf area. Rustic bar and seafaring atmosphere makes for high kitsch potential – but Pirates' Cove pulls it off. Fun and undemanding.

Amwaj (Hotel Inter-Continental Doha)
A huge buffet spread, open for breakfast, lunch and dinner with the possibility of dining outside on the pool terrace. Regular theme nights offer a choice of Arabic, Far-Eastern or Indian specialities, otherwise it's a mix of international favourites. Another venue for the family Friday brunch, a relaxed affair with clowns, candyfloss and popcorn for the children, very popular with local families.

Corniche Mediterranean (Doha Marriott)
Light, airy, fresh and contemporary, the ambiance in this outlet is relaxed and casual. Appealing to business people and families, locals, expatriate residents and visitors, the service offered is all-day dining from a range of changing buffets, each with a different national theme, and an à la carte menu.

Café Trottoir (Doha Marriott)
A European open-air café, indoors! Food and beverage service to a dedicated 36-seat courtyard setting and also the adjacent hotel lobby. Accommodating the varied tastes and cultures of the hotel and local clientele, the menu offers a wide selection of sweets, pastries and light snack foods and other savory items (including baguette sandwiches, mini-quiche, crepes, Belgium waffles and ice creams) along with alcoholic and non-alcoholic beverages, both hot and cold. Take-away service is also available.

Saloons, Bars and Pubs

Attitudes towards alcohol have changed over the last few years in Qatar. Even three years ago, having a drink was a slightly naughty affair, with bar areas unadvertised and hidden away in the darker reaches of hotels. Typical was the Ramada with its system of 'library tickets' discreetly issued to hotel residents by the concierge on the request of a hotel guest and presentation of a room key. The library ticket provided access to a rather sad night-club (in décor and layout only, once described as poorly lit, very un-cosy, in the style of early desperation) at which a glass of beer could be had. Nothing was advertised.

8

The good old days

More recently a knowing visitor to the Doha Sheraton (who had not been for a few years) checked in and, in true 'playing the game' British style murmured to the check-in clerk: 'Is it possible to have a drink here?' 'Yes sir', the clerk replied, 'go to the mezzanine floor and speak to the gentleman there.' Sure enough, outside the lift lobby was a man at a table, ledger akimbo. Following presentation of room number, the guest was motioned further down the corridor, which overlooked the vast hotel atrium. At the end of the second corridor were two tables and chairs. Promisingly, the table had beer mats on them. Eventually, a waiter appeared, 'Yes sir?' Making sure there were no ears to be offended the returnee again muttered discreetely: 'Um, yes. Two beers please'. The waiter looked surprised. 'You want them here, sir?' 'Is there anywhere else?' the guest replied. At which the waiter patiently responded, 'Most people go to the pub behind you, sir.

Today residents and visitors alike are spoilt for choice.

The Waterhole on the mezzanine at the Sheraton Doha is expanded around the corners. On one side of the L is a small restaurant area, while the other has seating and a big-screen TV. In between, a standing bar, dance floor and live music or disco for entertainment. Good food at reasonable prices but not suitable for a quiet drink. Similarly at the Ramada, Sheherazade (the name of the old night-club used for the library) has been very nicely rebuilt into a wooden-floored, inside bar with pool tables, dart boards, music and big-screen sports. It also has a fine outside balcony overlooking the rebuilt gardens and pool areas, which is a super place in the winter months for either a pub lunch or evening sun-downer. Other similar fare is to be had at the Poloma in the Inter-Continental and the sports bar at the top of the Marriott.

At the other end of the scale the Library (it still exists but is now on the top floor of the Ramada) is quiet and has great views over the city, with live music later in the evening. A popular spot to meet friends before or after a more formal evening elsewhere.

8

The Falcon lounge at the Ritz-Carlton has deep leather armchairs, cigars and cocktails. The Captain's Bar at the same hotel is good. For the best-value drinks in terms of price, the Oasis Hotel and Beach bar is probably the place to go.

Clubs

In covering food and drink we should not forget the clubs, which have also blossomed in the past few years. The Diplomatic Club just before you reach the Ritz Carlton, the Doha Golf Club and the Dana Club at the Khalifa Tennis and Squash complex all offer excellent meals and friendly bars or lounges. Membership is not necessary to enjoy the varied facilities on offer. The Golden Dragon Chinese restaurant located at the Dana Club should be singled out since it has recently changed hands and now offers not only first-class Chinese food but also Karaoke!

Other Restaurants

There are dozens and dozens of small restaurants in and around Doha, with more seeming to spring up by the day. Here are one or two suggestions:

Caravan Bukhara
❏ Tel: 444 0961

Part of the Sterling restaurant group, the Bukhara offers classic north Indian cuisine with mild and creamy curries, *tandooris*, *biriyanis* and freshly-baked Indian *naans* and *rotis*. They also do great Indian sweets. Located in the grounds of the Khalifa Tennis and Squash Club.

Shebastan Palace
❏ Tel: 432 4433

The Shabestan Palace is a personal favourite, with Iranian cuisine. All manner of kebabs and traditional accompaniments are on offer, prepared by Iranian chefs. Order a table in one of the alcoves for lunch with six or eight and ask for the mixed grill platter. Located on Al Sadd Street opposite Al Sadd Plaza.

Al Bandar Group of Restaurants
There is a cluster of restaurants at the Al Bandar complex on the Corniche immediately in front of the HSBC building. Right on the water, the complex houses the West Side steak house, a fish market, and Al Sharqui offering Oriental food. There are two coffee shops – one for families, the other for men. Sit out *al fresco* during the winter for lunch or even in the summer catch a cool breeze for dinner and admire the attractive lights around the Corniche.

Café Bateel
❏ Tel: 431 2313

Café Bateel is a good choice for a light snack and tea/coffee/soft drinks. It also has a good bakery. Its on Salwa Road between the MidMac roundabout and the Ramada Junction.

If you have a sweet tooth, try the Eli France Sweets and Coffee Shop, also on Salwa Road ❏ Tel: 431 2313 435 7111 and the City Centre shopping Mall. They specialise in French patisserie products and have rather elegant premises.

8

Fast Food

If you really are not the adventurous type or simply cannot make your mind up, then Doha offers everything that you are accustomed to at home, although often with a little more spice and a little more sweetness in the recipes. The Ramada Junction, or close to it, is where you will find just about one example of every big brand name available. Additional outlets are dotted around town so you will never be hungry, or slim. Doha's shopping malls all feature food-court outlets and a number of new malls are springing up.

8

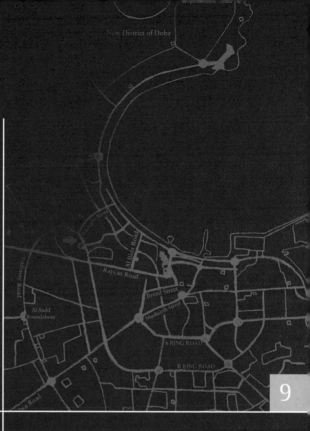

9

a break from business

a break from business

Doha is a small city and Qatar is a small country. But for the business visitor with a few hours of spare time, there is a surprising amount to see and do.

Before planning one's itinerary, though, it may be as well just to run through the ground rules:

• Ask permission before you take photographs of people. It is probably better not to attempt to take photos of elderly people and women. The same applies to members of the armed forces or the police. Also bear in mind that there are security sensitivities about photographing some public buildings, palaces, the airport, etc.
• Remember some of the little courtesies that are so vital in Qatar: right hand for eating, don't show the soles of your feet, 'please' and 'thank you' at all times. And smile!
• Don't forget that it's likely to be hot. Dress conservatively but in light clothing. Apply suncream and sunblock as appropriate. Hats are a good idea.
• Drink plenty of fluids. You dehydrate very quickly in the Gulf and an hour of strolling gently in the heat can be surprisingly debilitating.

Doha

The place to start is the Corniche. This seven-kilometre circular delight, with Palm Tree Island in the middle, stretches right from the Ras Abu Aboud flyover near the airport to the pyramid-shaped Sheraton Hotel West Bay. It is paved and landscaped and is hugely popular with the complete cross-section of Doha's inhabitants. It is thronged with people virtually from dawn until the early hours of the following morning. Serious sporting individuals and teams use it for training. Individuals, couples and groups stroll, meet, picnic or barbecue there. A cool breeze in the late summer night is welcome and the wide grassy edges form an ideal place to say prayers when the call is made. Old men sit and gossip while toddlers test their legs; bachelors come at the weekend for a look at the sights and have their photos taken next to the flowers and in front of the big buildings across the road, which they have perhaps had a hand in constructing. At night the lights of Doha are spectacular.

The Corniche is also used as a focal point for events and holiday spectaculars. At the drop of a hat fireworks displays are set off from Palm Tree Island. The entire Corniche, gardens and buildings are filled with displays

9

The Corniche

and lights during the *Eid* holidays. During these times fairs and circuses are mounted in the unused grounds near to the Central Post Office. Motor rallies and cycle races use the Corniche as a start and finish point, and sailors and jetskiers use the outer part of the bay.

Perhaps the highlight of a wander along the Corniche is the fishing marina, where the dhows and their doughty sailors meet, sit, make repairs, drink coffee and generally remind one of simpler times. Early in the morning the boats arrive with their catches, which can still be purchased (despite recent attempts to ban it) off the dockside.

In 2001 extensive work started on upgrading the Corniche itself and the adjoining facilities and parks on the opposite side of the busy main road. This work is carried out by the Ministry of Municipality and is part of an ongoing beautification plan.

Al Bida Park
Al Bida Park is a pleasant landscaped area on the Corniche between the National Theatre and the Ministry of Interior building. It features an art gallery, water features and fountains, shops and a café. There is also a children's mini-amusement park with rides and other attractions, skateboarding facilities and so on. Very popular as a family picnic site and often crowded in the evenings and at weekends.

Palm Tree Island

For an indulgent (and very touristy) Qatari experience, take a trip to Palm Tree Island. This exotic-sounding getaway has been open to the public since 1996. Ideal as a relaxing day-trip, or even as a venue for impressive corporate gatherings, this dream-like island has water sports, beach cabanas, restaurants and an abundance of palm trees. Dhows from the Corniche provide easy and frequent access to the island, which is open daily from 9.00 to 21.00. For information on bookings, contact:

❑ Tel: +974 869 151; fax: +974 865 202.

Further Afield
Sealine Beach Resort
Sealine Beach Resort is situated 55 km from Doha. Certainly worth a trip, this resort boasts a sea-view hotel, numerous sports and recreational activities as well as conference facilities and meeting rooms.

Visitors to the resort can pay daily rates of QR30, if not wanting to stay over. Hotel prices vary depending on preferred type of accommodation.

❏ Tel: 477 2722
E-mail: [sbr@qatar.net.qa]

The Doha Zoo

The Doha Zoo is not far from downtown Doha, lying only 15 km out of the city, on Salwa Road. It opens from 15.00 to 21.00 Sunday to Friday and provides entertainment to children as well as adults needing brief escapes from the corporate world!

Known as one of the loveliest beaches in the country, the Khor Al Udaid beach lies at the southeastern tip of Qatar, magnificent in its distinctive 40-metres-high sand dunes.

The Kingdom of Aladdin

The Kingdom of Aladdin (otherwise known as Entertainment City) is in the West Bay area. Open from Sunday to Friday, it offers children's play features, an artificial lagoon, a theatre and a cafeteria. Mondays and Wednesdays are dedicated to women and children under 12 only.

9

Forts and Museums

Al Koot Fort

Al Koot Fort is a white, Moorish fort in the middle of Doha. It houses a small exhibition of local handicrafts and is situated on the corner of Jassim bin Mohammed and Al Qalaa Streets. Open Sunday to Thursday 8.00-12.00 and 14.00-19.00.

Qatar National Museum

Qatar National Museum is a delightful, award-winning complex near the Corniche. The museum is housed in the restored Fariq Al Salata palace of Sheikh Abdullah bin Qassim and dates from 1901. The museum contains several notable collections of Bedouin culture, local costumes, jewelry, coins and weapons. There are also displays of perfumes and musical instruments. There are several informative display panels that discuss the ancient Arab knowledge of astronomy and other key sciences. A more modern side of Qatari life is explored in the upper floor display that shows how Qatar's oil and natural gas has been harvested. The cool of the evening is perhaps the best time to visit as a number of the artifacts are displayed in non air-conditioned rooms. Attached to the museum is a specialist maritime museum and a small but interesting aquarium where there are good displays of local and other fish. There is also a small lagoon where traditional Qatar-built boats are moored.

The Ethnographical Museum
The Ethnographical Museum is on Grand Hamad Street and is free of charge. It gives some insight into Qatar's history, being the last remaining construction of its kind in Doha.

Umm Slal Muhammad Fort
Umm Slal Muhammad Fort lies in the Umm Slal Mohammad area, 21 km from Doha. It is one of the residential forts that date from the late 19th century.

The Weaponry Museum
The Weaponry Museum displays samples of swords, daggers and miscellaneous firearms from bygone years. It is situated in Al Lagta, in Doha's suburban area. It is open from 09.00 to 12.00 and again from 15.00 to 18.00 every day except Friday and Saturday.

Other Towns and Locales
Since 86 per cent of Qatar's population lives in Doha or its near environs (Doha City 49 per cent, Al Rayan 32 per cent, Al Wakrah 5 per cent) it is natural that a good deal of the country's activity revolves around Doha and much of what you read refers to the capital. However there are a number of other towns worth visiting in the country.

Al Wakrah
Al Wakrah has been referred to by an enthusiastic young presenter on the radio as 'the second city'. With a population of 27,000 it is a substantial and growing satellite town halfway between Doha and the industrial town of Messaieed. Rental properties are cheaper than Doha and it is handy if one works in Messaieed. The population has increased some 60 per cent in four years, and the old fishing port has become the centre for booming commercial and fishing activities. The town is famous for its fine mosques and many houses reflecting the old Islamic architectural styles. There is also a museum displaying, among other things, traditional Arabic doors.

9

Al Khor
Al Khor lies 60 km to the north of Doha. Until the past century the town was a thriving port and pearl-fishing centre. Its fine mosques, museum housing valuable archeological pieces and acquisitions, and its historical towers are relics of the town's venerable history.

Messaieed
Umm Saieed is the name of the original village at the location and remains the name often used. Messaieed is situated south of Doha in the south-east of the country. Today it is a centre of heavy industry with a major seaport for oil exportation, and a commercial seaport.

Madinat Al-Shamal
A modern town functioning as an administrative centre for a number of coastal villages north of the country.

Dukhan
Dukhan was developed following the discovery of oil in the surrounding fields. Home of the oldest golf course in Qatar, which is financed by QP. This sand course has oiled fairways and browns (oiled sand) instead of greens. The hour's drive from Doha takes one through some remarkable desert including the wind-sculptured sand formations. The road, not particularly safe at present, will soon improve when the contract to develop it into a major highway is awarded. Dukhan is set to become something more than just an oil town as it will be close to the landing point of the Causeway link with Bahrain. Lovely beaches on the west coast will undoubtedly be opened as advanced tourism gets going.

9

Shahaniya
Shahaniya is west of Doha and has a purpose-built camel race track and is famed for the breeding of racing camels. Driving to Dukhan, one passes through the town and on either side can be seen strings of racing camels. Don't be shy of pulling off the road and exploring. Arab hospitality will always surface for the traveller.

Al-Zubara
This important archaeological site 105 km west of Doha was inhabited by many communities through history. Partial excavations at Al Zubara, which is on the north-east coast, have revealed foundations of city walls and

dwellings at several different levels. The fort, which now houses a regional museum, was built in 1938 during the reign of Sheikh Abdullah bin Qassim Al Thani and was used by the military until the mid 1980s.

Cinemas and Theatres

To find out what's on, call one of the following, all of which have multiple screens and show a number of different films at the same seating times:

Al Khaleej Cinema	❑ Tel: 467 1811
Doha Cinema	❑ Tel: 467 1811
The Mall Cinema	❑ Tel: 467 8888
Ameer Al Khaleej Cinema	❑ Tel: 442 4913

The two main theatres offer traditional Qatari productions as well as popular plays from other parts of the world. Contact details are:

Qatar National Theatre	❑ Tel: 483 1333
Doha Players Theatre	❑ Tel: 487 1196

9

Shopping

Qatar is the ideal place to spend a little time shopping. Whether it is for the cultural experience of browsing through traditional *suqs*, or simply to pick up some good deals on perfumes, electronics and jewellery, shopping is a typical activity when visiting Qatar.

Traditional Suqs

Suqs are clusters of small shops under the base of one roof, or sometimes standing together in outdoor areas. They make life easy by bunching all the shops offering similar products together. Selling everything from spices to fabrics to carpets to cameras, these traditional shops are still popular with all. Leave yourself plenty of time when you visit the *suqs*. The *suqs* are mainly bunched together in the centre of town just behind the Corniche, with another group just off the Salwa Road, about 20 minutes' drive from Doha's centre.

Here are some of the best-known *suqs* and what one may expect to find at each:

Suq Waqif

This is probably the oldest of the *suqs* and was the old weekend market for visiting Bedouin. One can obtain almost anything here including Qatari national dress, luggage, tools, general hardware, gardening equipment, tents, kitchenware, spices, incense and sweets.

Suq Ahmed
A modern two-floor structure in grey-and-white marble selling perfume (the real stuff mixed by the assistant) some electrical goods, ladies' tailors, ready-made clothing and fabrics.

The Gold *Suq*
Traditional gold jewellery, mostly 22 carat gold. It just sits there in great heaving lumps. Shop after shop. No armed guards. No double security doors. Pick it up and try it on. Feel the weight. Have it weighed. Buy it by weight at today's price per gram plus a percentage for workmanship. Gold is going up tomorrow, so buy it now!

Suq Nasser bin Saif
Another new structure specialising in electrical goods, CDs and audiotapes, plus clothing and children's toys.

Suq Asiery
When first built it was known as the Escalator *Suq* because it was the first to have one linking the two floors. The place to go for fabrics. You name it, they have it, or it's in their warehouse, which often happens to be the shop next door!

Suq Al Deira
The place for very exclusive designer, beaded, heavy lace fabrics. Not cheap, but you would be hard pressed to find cheaper in other countries, particularly European.

Central Markets
Third roundabout up from the Ramada roundabout along the Salwa Road will bring you to the Central Markets. Livestock (camels, goats, sheep), the fish market, the fruit and vegetable market, and nearby an open-air *suq* (like a European market with stalls). Don't forget to seek out the falcon *suq* at the back!

A Note on Bargaining
An essential tip for mastering *suq* shopping is to learn how to bargain! When visiting these traditional shops, it is expected that a great amount of haggling will take

place between traders and buyers. No trader ever believes that a customer will buy an item for its original sale price, and no customer should be so naïve as to accept one. The shopkeeper will be greatly disappointed if you don't ask for the best price or even one riyal off an item. Even if you are being asked five riyals, and you know it will cost you ten riyals back-home, bargain anyway. Not to do so will mean you have missed a large part of the fun of purchasing in the *suq*.

Shopping Complexes and Malls

There are an ever-growing number of Western style shopping centres, department stores and malls in Doha. All of them are proving to be popular amongst the various expatriate communities and locals alike and are reducing the need and pressure for expeditions to neighbouring countries (Dubai and Bahrain in particular). Only a few years ago these visits were not only eagerly welcomed as a means of getting a bit of rest and relaxation, but were necessary, since there was little to be had in Qatar.

These outlets can be grouped into two major categories – shopping centres and malls.

The first are primarily the older and established multi-product outlets and include Al Mana Centre, Blue Saloon, The Centre and Modern Company. All offer a range of goods on an open plan but mostly with minimal food-courts for eating and entertainment, if indeed any. Al Sadd Plaza, has been around for some time and since it did have a small supermarket and coffee shop could be better described as a mini-mall.

The new malls, offering every kind of service from food to clothing and entertainment, much of it through franchised outlets, are the Lamcy Centre, the Lulu Centre, the Mall, the Land Mark Centre, and of course the City Centre. More are being built and one wonders where all the shoppers are going to come from. However, one wondered the same in Dubai 20 years ago and now look at it! Opening times are 0900 to 1200 and 1600 to 2100, or even later. At some, Friday afternoons are dedicated to families which, loosely translated, means that a bachelor on his own is unlikely to be allowed beyond the supermarket areas. Men are allowed if they are accompanying their (or a) family group.

Sports

Qatar has gained something of a reputation as an ideal sporting country. In winter it has a clear and warm climate, attracting foreigners to sporting events held in the country.

Qatar hosts several annual international championships, all of which are supported and recognised by the appropriate international sporting bodies, such as the EPGA for golf, IIAF for athletics, ATP for Tennis and FIFA for football. Among these events are: the Qatar Open Tennis Tournament for men, Doha Masters Golf Tournament, Qatar Motor Rally, Athletics Grand Prix, Qatar Desert Horseracing Marathon and Arabian Horse Beauty Contests and Show Jumping and Dressage. Qatar also provided the first GCC States venue.

These events are rarely over-crowded with spectators. Local residents and visitors alike have a chance to rub shoulders with the world-class participants.

9

If you cannot get the timing right to attend an event, many of the venues and facilities are in regular use as clubs and are open for the use of visitors with the minimum of formalities.The Qatar Masters Golf Tournament is held annually in March at the Doha Golf Club, a club beautifully maintained and priced to match it!

❑ Tel: 483 2338

The Rayan Racing and Equestrian Club organises Qatar's racing season which runs from October to April and includes events such as the Emiri Sword event and the Qatar International Desert Marathon. This is a popular Qatari sport, although it has not really caught on amongst many expatriates yet.

Fishing trips are popular with visitors to Qatar. The hotels, run by smart businessmen, offer daily or hourly trips including picnic lunches, at marked-up prices. Certainly a vital Qatari experience, fishing will, however be cheaper if organised through individual means.

Sailing is obviously a major sport in Qatar. The Doha Sailing Association offers dinghies and windsurfers to anyone interested in hiring them. The Regatta Sailing School Academy provides lessons for all levels, and is located at the Sheraton Hotel. ❑ Tel: 442 4577 to book lessons.

Water-skiing is not the only kind of skiing to take place in Qatar. Khor Al-Udaid, situated 78 km southeast of Doha, boasts sand dunes reaching up to heights of 40m, offering sand skiing alongside various watersports.

The Doha Golf Club

Situated in the West Bay Lagoons, the Doha Golf Club has one of the most spectacular sea views of the Arabian Sea. Peter Harradine's design of the course has left it looking natural and scattered with palm trees, cacti (some are local whilst the big ones are imported from Arizona) and shrubs, not to mention eight salt or freshwater lakes, some of which are stocked with enormous Koi Carp.

The standard of golf on this course is high, as golfers have to deal with a technically tricky course as well as persistent sea breezes constantly from the coast. Seven of the course's holes incorporate water of some kind, while the rest are surrounded by desert!

Next to the Championship Course is a nine-hole Academy Course, suitable for beginners and those wanting a relaxing social game of golf.

Recreational Clubs

Although most recreational clubs in Qatar that are not a part of a hotel are designed specifically for members, most offer daily rates to visitors.

Doha Club in the Abu Aboud area overlooks the Gulf water front and offers fantastic facilities including a beautiful beach, enormous swimming pool, squash courts and tennis courts as well as a private marina.

❏ Tel: 441 8822

The Diplomatic Club lies in the West Bay and offers its members spectacular facilities including a businessman's meeting hall and an all-purpose hall which holds up to 400 people. A library, beauty centre, restaurants and tennis and squash courts are also offered to members of this club.

❏ Tel: 444 3743

Cultural Activities

Cine-Club

Every Wednesday night at 20.00, French films are shown at the Sofitel Hotel. Anyone is welcome to attend these, whether they are staying at the hotel or not.

❏ Tel: 443 5222 for details.

Ceramics making
Ideal for the businessman's spouse or children, Ceramics Galore offers classes, expertly guiding one through the art of creating one's own ceramics. Contact Ceramics Galore on ❏ Tel: 483 3874 to book a lesson or just to browse through and admire the creations of others.

Boat trips
While fishing trips might suit the more adventurous, a more leisurely occupation is the option of a boat trip from the Corniche. Organised through the Doha Marriott or the Doha Club, these traditional Qatari excursions cost QR10 for adults or QR5 for children.

Outward Bound
Khor Al Udaid
The Inland Sea in the south-east is surrounded by spectacular crescent-shaped sand dunes. An area of outstanding beauty appreciated by photographers for the changing light and colours at different times of the day. A four-wheel drive is essential, and go with someone who knows the route. Alternatively, tour operators organise day trips and overnight camps and provide picnics and barbecues, folkloric entertainment and sometimes the opportunity to ride camels and go sand-skiing. One 'folkloric' event in the area used to be the local lads taking their brand new four-wheel-drive cars on a Friday afternoon jaunt up or across an enormous, near-vertical, sand dune wall at high speed for the delight of the gathered spectators. The inevitable accidents, to both participants and sometimes spectators, caused the authorities to bring it to a stop.

Beaches
Qatar has numerous sheltered beaches with sandy shores and shallow seas. Among the most popular are at Al Wakrah near the fishing village and Al Khor with its own Corniche and undeveloped beaches south of the town. In the north-east of the country there are undeveloped beaches at Sumaismah, Fuwairit, and Al Ghariya, whilst travelling south one finds beaches at Messaieed and Khor Al Udaid. Better to go with friends and residents of Qatar who know the way around and have sampled the best locations.

9

Jebel Jassassiyeh Carvings

A rocky ridge close to the coast just north of Al Huwailah is covered in rock carvings thought to date back thousands of years. There are more than 900 carvings, which depict different types of boats as seen from both elevation and plan. Rows of rosettes or cup-marks were used for traditional games called Al Aailah and Al Haloosah, which were played using stones. These carvings were first catalogued in 1974 and are considered the most significant of several similar sites in the country.

Desert driving

As you will have gathered Qatar is not overdeveloped: stark and barren is a better description, when you get off the beaten track, which is very easy to do.

To reach many of the interesting places mentioned above, especially the undeveloped beaches, it is necessary to go off-road. A few words of advice are therefore not amiss, and these should be well understood, remembered and heeded, even if you actually have no intention of driving in the desert.

Don't think of driving in the desert unless you have a four-wheel-drive car. Experience is essential and it is inadvisable to set off through the desert on one's own.

● Always go with at least one other car, and better still, go with an old hand who has done that sort of thing before.

● Never drive after sunset (16.45 in winter)

● Tyre pressure should ideally be between 18 and 20 psi on all tyres.

● Be prepared for wear and tear to the vehicle! (Usually about 500-100 kms worth of wear and tear per day, and that's for a good driver.)

● Never set off without essentials, such as sunscreen, drinking water (lots of it), fully charged mobile phone, compass, first-aid kit, spare tyre and means of reflating the tyres when you do back to a road (pump and money for the gas station if they have a compressor.. air is not free) and boards for propping jacks and other equipment in soft sand.

● Make sure someone knows your intended route and probable return time.

● If you do get stranded DO NOT LEAVE THE VEHICLE.

Many books are available on desert driving. The best is Jim Stabler's *The Desert Driver's Manual*.

9

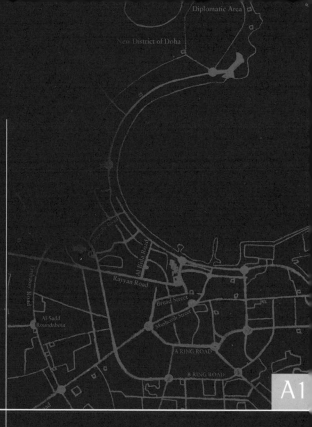

Appendix One

A1

appendix one

Useful phone numbers

Below is a directory of useful telephone numbers in Qatar. All Qatari numbers are 7 digits long. Fixed numbers begin with a 4, and mobiles begin with a 5. Pagers (or 'bleep' numbers) begin with a 2.
To dial internationally from Qatar, dial 0 + country code + required number. Reduced rates apply on Fridays, public holidays and between 19.00 and 7.00.
To dial Qatar from abroad, the country code is +974

Emergencies

Police, Fire, Ambulance 999

Hospitals

Hamad Hospital	**t:** 439 2111
HMC Accident & Emergency	**t:** 439 2222
Rumailah Hospital	**t:** 439 3333
Women's Hospital Emergency	**t:** 439 4444
American Hospital	**t:** 442 4888
Qatar Medical Centre	**t:** 444 0606
Doha Clinic Hospital	**t:** 432 7300
Doha Dental Centre	**t:** 467 5225
Doha Chiropractic Centre	**t:** 467 6849

A1

Hotels

Hotel Inter-Continental Doha	**t:** 484 4444
The Ritz-Carlton	**t:** 484 8000
Doha Marriott Gulf Hotel	**t:** 443 2432
Sheraton Doha Hotel & Resort	**t:** 485 4444
Ramada Hotel	**t:** 441 7417
Sealine Beach Resort (Messaieed)	**t:** 477 2722
Sofitel Hotel Doha Palace	**t:** 443 5222
Mövenpick Hotel Doha	**t:** 429 1111
The Oasis Hotel & Beach Club	**t:** 442 4424

Smaller Hotels

New Doha Palace Hotel	**t:** 442 6131
Regency Hotel	**t:** 436 3363
Shezan Hotel & Restaurant	**t:** 486 5225
Al Bustan Hotel	**t:** 432 8888

Airports

Doha airport	**t:** 465 6660
Air traffic enquiries	**t:** 462 2999

Airlines

Air France	*t:* 432 0802
Air India	*t:* 432 4111
Biman Bangladesh	*t:* 441 3422
British Airways	*t:* 432 1434
Cyprus Airways	*t:* 441 8666
Egypt Air	*t:* 445 8302
Emirates	*t:* 441 8877
Gulf Air	*t:* 445 5444
KLM	*t:* 432 1208
Kuwait Airways	*t:* 443 5340
Pakistan International Airlines	*t:* 442 6290
Qatar Airways	*t:* 449 6666
Royal Jordanian	*t:* 443 1431
Saudi Arabian	*t:* 432 2991
Sri Lankan	*t:* 444 1161

Travel Agencies

Ali Bin Ali Travel Bureau	*t:* 444 1161
Cleopatra Travels	*t:* 443 9333
Darwish Travel & Tourism	*t:* 442 2411
Darwish Travel Bureau	*t:* 441 8666
Qatar Travels	*t:* 442 8001
Qatar Tours	*t:* 441 1414
Rayan Travel	*t:* 441 8587
Regency Travel & Tourist	*t:* 444 3444
Tourist Travel Bureau	*t:* 444 7499

Telecommunications

Telephone directory	180
Telephone assistance (local)	100
International calls - enquiries	190
International calls - bookings	150
Speaking clock (English)	140
Speaking clock (Arabic)	141
Telegram Enquiries	130

Courier Services

Aramex	*t:* 442 6101
DHL	*t:* 462 1202
Federal Express	*t:* 466 1722
TNT Express Worldwide	*t:* 462 2262
UPS	*t:* 432 2444
Skynet	*t:* 443 1122
WGA	*t:* 441 2881

A1

Credit Card Emergencies

Amex	**t:** +44 1273 696933
Diners Club	**t:** 439 596
Visa	**t:** +1 410 581 9091

Car Rentals

Avis	**t:** 466 7744
Budget	**t:** 441 9500
Europcar	**t:** 443 8404
Hertz	**t:** 462 2891
National Car Rental	**t:** 487 1995
Al Muftah Rent a Car	**t:** 432 8100
Prestige Rent a Car	**t:** 483 8500

Banks

Al Ahli Bank of Qatar	**t:** 432 6611
Grindlays Qatar Bank	**t:** 447 3700
Arab Bank Ltd.	**t:** 443 7979
Bank Saderat Iran	**t:** 441 4646
Banque Paribas	**t:** 443 3844
Commercial Bank of Qatar	**t:** 449 0222
Doha Bank	**t:** 445 6600
HSBC Bank Middle East	**t:** 441 3213
Qatar International Islamic Bank	**t:** 440 9409
Qatar National Bank	**t:** 440 7407
Standard Chartered Bank	**t:** 441 4252
Union Bank	**t:** 443 8666
Central Bank of Qatar	**t:** 4456456
Mashreq Bank	**t:** 4413213
Qatar Industrial Development Bank	**t:** 4421600

A1

Prominent Exchange Houses

Al Sadd Exchange	**t:** 432 3334
Al Fardan Exchange	**t:** 440 8408
Al Mana Exchange	**t:** 442 4226
City Exchange	**t:** 441 4632
Eastern Exchange	**t:** 441 2655
Gulf Exchange	**t:** 442 1744
Habib Qatar International Exchange	
	t: 442 4373
Islamic Exchange	**t:** 442 2718
Trust Exchange	**t:** 435 2055
Union Exchange	**t:** 442 3715

Embassies

Algeria	*t:* 483 1186
Bahrain	*t:* 483 9360
Bangladesh	*t:* 467 1927
Bosnia Herzegovina	*t:* 467 0194
Brunei	*t:* 483 1956
China	*t:* 488 4202
Cuba	*t:* 467 2072
Egypt	*t:* 483 2555
Eritrea	*t:* 466 7934
France	*t:* 483 2283
Gambia	*t:* 465 1429
Germany	*t:* 487 6959
India	*t:* 467 2021
Indonesia	*t:* 465 7945
Iran	*t:* 483 5300
Iraq	*t:* 467 2237
Italy	*t:* 466 7842
Japan	*t:* 483 1224
Jordan	*t:* 483 2238
Kuwait	*t:* 483 2111
Lebanon	*t:* 447 7773
Libyan Brotherhood Bureau	*t:* 466 7206
Mauritania	*t:* 483 6003
Morocco	*t:* 483 1885
Nepal	*t:* 467 5681
Oman	*t:* 467 0744
Pakistan	*t:* 483 2525
Palestine	*t:* 442 2531
Philippines	*t:* 483 1585
Romania	*t:* 468 3777
Russia	*t:* 432 9117
Saudi Arabia	*t:* 483 2030
Senegal	*t:* 467 6587
Somalia	*t:* 483 2771
Sri Lanka	*t:* 467 7627
Sudan	*t:* 466 0207
Syria	*t:* 483 1844
Tunisia	*t:* 483 2646
Turkey	*t:* 483 5204
United Arab Emirates	*t:* 483 8880
United Kingdom	*t:* 442 1991
United States of America	*t:* 488 4101
Yemen	*t:* 443 2555

A1

Appendix Two

A2

Appendix two

Arabic Language

The Arabic language exists in its purist from in the words of the Quran, and this written Arabic, known as Classical Arabic (Fusha) has a much-studied structure and grammar, acknowledged by the Arabs themselves as highly complex. Mastery of classical Arabic is a highly respected skill.

Modern spoken Arabic, although building upon the principles of classical Arabic, has evolved into regional dialects, varying across the different parts of the Arab world but normally comprehensible to all.

The following are a few essential phrases of standard Gulf Arabic, and should help to get you through the courtesies.

Basic conventions

Arabic contains some consonants which do not exist in the Roman script, but can be approximated to the following sounds

A2

Kha	like 'ch' in the Scottish word *loch*
Gh	like a rolled French 'r', sometimes described as akin to a gargle at the back of the throat
'ein	A glottal stop, as in the cockney 'water', i.e. *wa'er*

Stressed syllables are marked in bold.

Useful phrases

Good morning	Sa**baah** al-**khair**
Reply (morning of light)	Sa**baah** an- **noor**
Good evening	Ma**saa** al-**khair**
Reply (evening of light)	Ma**saa** an-**noor**
Good night	**Tis**bah'ala **khair**
Greetings (peace be with you)	Assa**lam** a**lai**kum
Reply (peace be upon you too)	Wa a**lai**kum assa**lam**
Hello	**Mar**haba
How are you ?	Kayf **Ha**lak? or **Kay**fak? (**kay**fik? to a

woman)

Very well	**Bikhayr** (followed by)
Praise be to God	Al-**ham**du lil**lah**
Welcome (said by host)	**Ah**lan wa-sahlan
Reply	**Ah**lan **bik**um
God willing	**In**shallah

(It is the convention to say this whenever referring to any future event)

Goodbye (the one leaving)	**Ma**'a sa**lam**a
Goodbye (the one remaining)	Fi i**man** al**lah**

Making conversation

My name is Andrew	**Is**mi Andrew
And what is your name?	Waish **Is**mak?
Pleased to have met you	Fursa saeeda

(lit.' It was a fortunate chance')

Honestly	Wal**lah**i

(frequently used for emphasis)

Do you speak English?	**Int** tata**kal**am Ingleesi?
I do not speak Arabic	La ata**kall**um '**Ar**abi
I am American	**An**a Amreeki
I am British	**An**a Ingleesi
I am French	**An**a Faransi
I am German	**An**a Al**maan**i
I am Swedish	**An**a Su**wei**di

Please (general use)	Law samaht
Please (formal)	Min **fad**lak (Min **Fadh**lik to a woman)
Thank you	**Shuk**ran
Thank you very much	**Shuk**ran jazeelan
Many thanks	Alf **shoukr**
Excuse me	**Aff**wan
After you	Ta**fadh**al (Taf**fadh**ali to a woman)

How?	Kayf?
How much?	**Bik**am?
How many?	Kam?
Who?	Meen?
What?	Aish?
What is this?	Aish **Had**ha?
What's the problem?	**Aish** al-mushkila?
There's no problem	**Ma** fi mushkila

What do you want?	Aish **Tib**gha?
When?	**Mata**?
Where?	Wayn?
Why?	Laysh?
Here	**Hi**na
There	**Hin**ak
Is it possible?	**Mum**kin?
OK	Tamaam or **Tay**yib or Zayn
Yes	Na'am or Aiwa
No	La

Numbers

Zero	**Si**fir
One	**Wa**hid
Two	Ithn**ayn**
Three	Tha**la**tha
Four	**Ar**ba'a
Five	**Kham**sa
Six	**Sit**ta
Seven	**Sab**'a
Eight	Tha**ma**nia
Nine	**Tis**'a
Ten	**'Ash**ra
Eleven	**Had**-Ashr
Twelve	**Itn**a-Ashr
Thirteen	T**a**lat-Ashr
Fourteen	**'Ar**bat-Ashr
Fifteen	**Kham**sat-Ashr
Sixteen	**Sit**ta-Ashr
Seventeen	**Sab**a'at-Ashr
Eighteen	**Tam**ant- Ashr
Nineteen	**Tis**ea'at-Ashr
Twenty	**'Ash**reen
Thirty	T**a**lateen
Forty	**Arb**aean
Fifty	**Kham**seen
Sixty	**Sit**teen
Seventy	**Sab**a'een
Eighty	**Tam**aneen
Ninety	**Tis**een
One hundred	**Ma**ya
One thousand	Alf
Two thousand	Alf**ayn**

A2

Ten thousand	Ashrat alaaf
One million	Malion
Billion	Miliar
Once	Marra
Twice	Marratayn
Three times	Talat marraat
First	Awwal
Second	Thani
Last	Akheer
Where is?	Ween?
Entrance	Madkhal
Grocery store	Baqala
Hospital	Mustashfa
Library	Maktaba
Museum	Mathaf
Office	Maktab
Chemist	Saidaliya
Police Station	Markaz as-shourta
Post Office	Markaz al-bareed
Restaurant	Mat'am
Railway Station	Mahatat Qitar
How much is?	Bikam?
Do you have...?	Hal 'andak...?
Blouse	Blooza
Dress	Fistan
Nightshirt	Qamees an-nawm
Shirt	Qamees
Shoes	Jazma
Long skirt	Tannoura
Socks	Sharab
Lipstick	Rouj
Perfume	Riha
Colours	
Black	Aswad
Blue	Azraq
Brown	Bunni
Green	Akhdar
Red	Ahmar
Yellow	Assfar
White	Abyad

Common Adjectives

Large	Kabir
Long	Taweel
Small	Saghir
Short	Qasir

Negatives

I do not want	Ma abgha
I do not have	Ma 'andi
I don't know	Ma adri

Instructions

Look	Shoof
Give me	Ateeni
Go away	Ruh/Imshee
Hurry up	Bi sur'ah
Stop	Waqif
Never mind	La yahim or Ma yahim
Again	Marra Thaniah
Everything	Kull shai
All of us	Kulluna
Together	Ma'a ba'adh
Later	Ba'adayn

Time

Minute	Dageega
Hour	Sa'a
What time is it?	Kam essa'a?
It's two thirty	Essa'a ithnayn w'noss
Eight o'clock	Essa'a thamania
Quarter to ten	'Ashra illa rub'a
Quarter past three	Essa'a thalatha wa rub

Days

What day is it?	Waish al-yawm?
Monday	Yawm al-ithnayn
Tuesday	Yawm al-thalath
Wednesday	Yawm al-'arbi'a
Thursday	Yawm al-khamis
Friday	Yawm al-juma'a
Saturday	Yawm as-sabt
Sunday	Yawm al-ahad

A2

Money

Where can I change some money?	**Wayn** agh**ayir** al-'**um**la?
There at the Bank	Hinaak fil **bank**
Is there a bank at the airport?	Fi **bank** fil ma**t**ar?
Yes, over there	Naam, **hu**wa hinaak

Accommodation

Hotel	**Fun**duk
I have a reservation for one room	'**An**di **ha**jz li **ghur**fa wa**hi**da
I need a quiet room	**Ab**ga **ghur**fa ha**di**ya
I need the room for two days	**Ab**ga al-**ghur**fa li yaw**mayn**.
I need the room for one week	**Ab**ga al-**ghur**fa li usbu'ah
Single or double bed?	Bi-sareer **wa**had aw sareer**ayn**?
Room with a double bed, please	**Ghor**fa bi sirareer**ayn** law sa**maht**
How much per night?	Kam **sir**'a li **lai**la?
OK that's fine	**Ta**yyib, **he**dha **zein**
May I have the bill	Al-fa**too**ra law sa**maht**
Thank you for the good service	**Shuk**ran lil **khi**dma al-mumtaaza

Food

Restaurant	**mat**'an
What would you like to eat?	Waish **tib**gha **ta**kul?
Would you please bring some,	Law sa**maht** **jib**lee..

The menu	**Waj**bah
Bananas .	Mooz
Bread	Khobz or Aish
Butter	**Zib**da
Chicken	Da**jaj**
Coffee	**Gah**wa
Corn	**Dhur**rah
Cucumber	Khi**yar**
Dates	**Ta**mar
Garlic	Toum
Grapes	'**ai**nab
Lamb	**La**ham kha**roof**
Lettuce	Khass
Fresh milk	Ha**leeb**
Olives	Zay**toun**

A2

Onions	**Bas**al
Rice	Ruzz
Roast Beef	**Laham mash**wee
Salt	Milh
Soup	**Shor**ba
Steak	Steak
Sugar	**Suk**kar
Tomatoes	**Tamat**im
Vegetables	Khu**daar**
Vinegar	Khall
Water	**Mai**ya

A2

appendix three
commercial support
for US companies

A3

A3

Appendix three

Directory of Export Assistance Centers

Cities in capital letters are centres which combine the export promotion and trade finance service of the Department of Commerce, the Export-Import Bank, the Small Business Administration and the Agency of International Development.

Two of the largest and most useful export associations in the US are ExportZone U.S.A. and The Export Institute of the U.S.

ExportZone U.S.A.
218 W. San Marcos Blvd
Suite # 106-176
San Marcos, CA 92069
U.S.A.
q Tel: 760 295 1652; fax: 760 295 1656
E-mail: [info@exportzone.com]

&

The Export Institute of the United States of America
6901 W.84th St., Suite 359
Minneapolis, MN 55438
Tel: 800 943 3171; fax: 952 943 1535
Email: [jrj@exportinstitute.com]

A3

ALABAMA
Birmingham, Alabama - George Norton, Director
950 22nd Street North, Room 707, ZIP 35203
t: : (205) 731-1331   *f:* (205) 731-0076

ALASKA
Anchorage, Alaska - Charles Becker, Director
550 West 7th Ave., Suite 1770, ZIP: 99501
t: (907) 271-6237   *f:* (907) 271-6242

ARIZONA
Phoenix, Arizona - Frank Woods, Director
2901 N. Central Ave., Suite 970, ZIP 85012
t: (602) 640-2513   *f:* (602) 640-2518

CALIFORNIA - LONG BEACH
Joseph F Sachs, Director
Mary Delmege, CS Director
One World Trade Center, Ste. 1670, ZIP: 90831
t: (562) 980-4550   *f:* (562) 980-4561

CALIFORNIA - SAN JOSE
101 Park Center Plaza, Ste. 1001, ZIP: 95113
t: (408) 271-7300   *f:* (408) 271-7307

COLORADO - DENVER
Nancy Charles-Parker, Director
1625 Broadway, Suite 680, ZIP: 80202
t: (303) 844-6623   *f:* (303) 844-5651

CONNECTICUT
Middletown, Connecticut - Carl Jacobsen, Director
213 Court Street, Suite 903 ZIP: 06457-3346
t: (860) 638-6950   *f:* (860) 638-6970

DELAWARE
Served by the Philadelphia, Pennsylvania U.S. Export
Assistance Center

FLORIDA - MIAMI
John McCartney, Director
P.O. Box 590570, ZIP: 33159
5600 Northwest 36th St., Ste. 617, ZIP: 33166
t: (305) 526-7425   *f:* (305) 526-7434

GEORGIA - ATLANTA
Samuel Troy, Director
285 Peachtree Center Avenue, NE, Suite 200
ZIP: 30303-1229
t: (404) 657-1900   *f:* (404) 657-1970

HAWAII
Honolulu, Hawaii - Greg Wong, Manager
1001 Bishop St.; Pacific Tower; Suite 1140
ZIP: 96813
t: (808) 522-8040   *f:* (808) 522-8045

IDAHO
Boise, Idaho - James Hellwig, Manager
700 West State Street, 2nd Floor, ZIP: 83720
t: (208) 334-3857   *f:* (208) 334-2783

ILLINOIS - CHICAGO
Mary Joyce, Director
55 West Monroe Street, Suite 2440, ZIP: 60603
t: (312) 353-8045   *f:* (312) 353-8120

A3

INDIANA
Indianapolis, Indiana - Dan Swart, Manager
11405 N. Pennsylvania Street, Suite 106
Carmel, IN, ZIP: 46032
t: (317) 582-2300   *f:* (317) 582-2301

IOWA
Des Moines, Iowa - Allen Patch, Director
601 Locust Street, Suite 100, ZIP: 50309-3739
t: (515) 288-8614   *f:* (515) 288-1437

KANSAS
Wichita, Kansas - George D. Lavid, Manager
209 East William, Suite 300, ZIP: 67202-4001
t: (316) 269-6160   *f:* (316) 269-6111

KENTUCKY
Louisville, Kentucky - John Autin, Director
601 W. Broadway, Room 634B , ZIP: 40202
t: (502) 582-5066   *f:* (502) 582-6573

LOUISIANA
Patricia Holt, Acting Director
365 Canal Street, Suite 1170
New Orleans ZIP: 70130
t: (504) 589-6546   *f:* (504) 589-2337

MAINE
Portland, Maine - Jeffrey Porter, Manager
c/o Maine International Trade Center
511 Congress Street, ZIP: 04101
t: (207) 541-7400   *f:* (207) 541-7420

MARYLAND - BALTIMORE
Michael Keaveny, Director
World Trade Center, Suite 2432
401 East Pratt Street, ZIP: 21202
t: (410) 962-4539   *f:* (410) 962-4529

MASSACHUSETTS - BOSTON
Frank J. O'Connor, Director
164 Northern Avenue
World Trade Center, Suite 307, ZIP: 02210
t: (617) 424-5990   *f:* (617) 424-5992

A3

MICHIGAN - DETROIT
Neil Hesse, Director
211 W. Fort Street, Suite 2220, ZIP: 48226
t: (313) 226-3650   *f:* (313) 226-3657

MINNESOTA - MINNEAPOLIS
Ronald E. Kramer, Director
45 South 7th St., Suite 2240, ZIP: 55402
t: (612) 348-1638   *f:* (612) 348-1650

MISSISSIPPI
Mississippi - Harrison Ford, Manager
704 East Main St., Raymond, MS, ZIP: 39154
t: (601) 857-0128   *f:* (601) 857-0026

MISSOURI - ST LOUIS
Randall J. LaBounty, Director
8182 Maryland Avenue, Suite 303, ZIP: 63105
t: (314) 425-3302   *f:* (314) 425-3381

MONTANA
Missoula, Montana - Mark Peters, Manager
c/o Montana World Trade Center
Gallagher Business Bldg., Suite 257, ZIP: 59812
t: (406) 243-2098   *f:* (406) 243-5259

NEBRASKA
Omaha, Nebraska - Meredith Bond, Manager
11135 "O" Street, ZIP: 68137
t: (402) 221-3664   *f:* (402) 221-3668

NEVADA
Reno, Nevada - Jere Dabbs, Manager
1755 East Plumb Lane, Suite 152, ZIP: 89502
t: (702) 784-5203   *f:* (702) 784-5343

NEW HAMPSHIRE
Portsmouth, New Hampshire - Susan Berry, Manager
17 New Hampshire Avenue, ZIP: 03801-2838
t: (603) 334-6074   *f:* (603) 334-6110

NEW JERSEY
Trenton, New Jersey - Rod Stuart, Director
3131 Princeton Pike, Bldg. #4, Suite 105, ZIP: 08648

A3

t: (609) 989-2100   *f:* (609) 989-2395

NEW MEXICO
New Mexico - Sandra Necessary, Manager
c/o New Mexico Dept. of Economic Development
P.O. Box 20003, Santa Fe, ZIP: 87504-5003
FEDEX:1100 St. Francis Drive, ZIP: 87503
t: (505) 827-0350   *f:* (505) 827-0263

NEW YORK
t: (212) 466-5222   *f:* (212) 264-1356

NORTH CAROLINA
Roger Fortner, Director
521 East Morehead Street, Suite 435, Charlotte,
ZIP: 28202
t: (704) 333-4886   *f:* (704) 332-2681

NORTH DAKOTA
Served by the Minneapolis, Minnesota Export
Assistance Center

OHIO - CLEVELAND
Michael Miller, Director
600 Superior Avenue, East, Suite 700
ZIP: 44114
t: (216) 522-4750   *f:* (216) 522-2235

OKLAHOMA
Oklahoma City, Oklahoma - Ronald L. Wilson, Director
301 Northwest 63rd Street, Suite 330, ZIP: 73116
t: (405) 608-5302   *f:* (405) 608-4211

OREGON - PORTLAND
Scott Goddin, Director
One World Trade Center, Suite 242
121 SW Salmon Street, ZIP: 97204
t: (503) 326-3001   *f:* (503) 326-6351

PENNSYLVANIA - PHILADELPHIA
Rod Stuart, Acting Director
615 Chestnut Street, Ste. 1501, ZIP: 19106
t: (215) 597-6101   *f:* (215) 597-6123

A3

PUERTO RICO
San Juan, Puerto Rico (Hato Rey) - Vacant, Manager
525 F.D. Roosevelt Avenue, Suite 905
ZIP: 00918
t: (787) 766-5555   *f:* (787) 766-5692

RHODE ISLAND
Providence, Rhode Island - Vacant, Manager
One West Exchange Street, ZIP: 02903
t: (401) 528-5104, *f:* (401) 528-5067

SOUTH CAROLINA
Columbia, South Carolina - Ann Watts, Director
1835 Assembly Street, Suite 172, ZIP: 29201
t: (803) 765-5345   *f:* (803) 253-3614

SOUTH DAKOTA
Siouxland, South Dakota - Cinnamon King, Manager
Augustana College, 2001 S. Summit Avenue
Room SS-44, Sioux Falls, ZIP: 57197
t: (605) 330-4264   *f:* (605) 330-4266

TENNESSEE
Memphis, Tennessee - Ree Russell, Manager
Buckman Hall, 650 East Parkway South, Suite 348
ZIP: 38104.
t: (901) 323-1543   *f:* (901) 320-9128

TEXAS - DALLAS
 LoRee Silloway, Director
P.O. Box 420069, ZIP: 75342-0069
2050 N. Stemmons Fwy., Suite 170, ZIP: 75207
t: (214) 767-0542   *f:* (214) 767-8240

UTAH
Salt Lake City, Utah - Stanley Rees, Director
324 S. State Street, Suite 221, ZIP: 84111
t: (801) 524-5116   *f:* (801) 524-5886

VERMONT
Montpelier, Vermont - Susan Murray, Manager
National Life Building, Drawer 20, ZIP: 05620-0501
t: (802) 828-4508   *f:* (802) 828-3258

A3

VIRGINIA
Richmond, Virginia - Helen D. Lee Hwang, Manager
400 North 8th Street, Suite 540, ZIP: 23240-0026
P.O. Box 10026
t: (804) 771-2246   **f:** (804) 771-2390

WASHINGTON - SEATTLE
David Spann, Director
2001 6th Ave, Suite 650, ZIP: 98121
t: (206) 553-5615   **f:** (206) 553-7253

WEST VIRGINIA
Charleston, West Virginia - Harvey Timberlake, Director
405 Capitol Street, Suite 807, ZIP: 25301
t: (304) 347-5123   **f:** (304) 347-5408

WISCONSIN
Milwaukee, Wisconsin - Paul D. Churchill, Director
517 E. Wisconsin Avenue, Room 596, ZIP: 53202
t: (414) 297-3473   **f:** (414) 297-3470

WYOMING
Served by the Denver, Colorado U.S. Export Assistance
Center

A3

Gorilla Guides

128 Kensington Church Street, London W8 4BH
Tel: (44) 207 221 7166; Fax: (44) 207 792 9288
E-mail: enquiries@stacey-international.co.uk
Website: www.stacey-international.co.uk

business travellers'
HANDBOOKS

The series that focuses on the needs of the business traveller

The Series

- **Unique:** Nothing like this currently available in the trade market
- **Recognised:** Already widely accepted as the reference by some chambers of commerce and export desks of The Department of Trade and Industry
- **Authoritative:** Highly experienced authors with extensive business experience in the target market

The Business Travellers' Guides to

- **Turkey**
- **Egypt**
- **Argentina**
- **The United Arab Emirates**
- **Saudi Arabia**
- **Qatar**
- **Lebanon**
- **China**

Content

- **Quality and Efficiency:** Essential tips on where to stay and how to get started
- **Etiquette:** The social morés of the local business culture
- **Creating an Impression:** Where to lunch and dine a local guest; basic vocabulary and phrases
- **The nitty-gritty:** Full details of organisations offering support and advice
- **Business Overviews:** Authoritative insights into the major economic and commercial sectors
- **Contacts:** Appendixes of useful contact details